COMING HOME

Discipleship, Ecology and Everyday Economics

JONATHAN CORNFORD

MORNING STAR PUBLISHING

Published in Australia by
Morning Star Publishing
P. O. Box 462
Reservoir Vic. 3073
Australia

ISBN 9780648453727

Cataloguing-in-Publication entry is available from the National Library of Australia http://catalogue.nla.gov.au.

This edition first published in 2019

Typesetting by John Healy

For Kim

who has been my collaborator and companion on this adventure,
and whose grace makes it all possible.

CONTENTS

PREFACE & ACKNOWLEDGEMENTS

This book has been inspired by the Sevenfold Household Covenant developed by Bartimaeus Cooperative Ministries in the USA and more generally by the Sabbath Economics work of Ched Myers from Bartimaeus. The Sevenfold Covenant was developed as a tool for helping people to translate a biblical perspective on economics into their own economic lives. When I began Manna Gum as a ministry in 2009,[1] I adapted this tool for an Australian context, calling it simply 'the Household Covenant'. I began running seven-week Bible studies for groups of between 10 to 20 people and found the process invaluable as, again and again, I was hearing that people had never read the Bible in this way before. More than that, they found that putting the work in to clarify what the Bible taught on various issues of economic life was profoundly useful for disentangling some of the moral, existential and lifestyle challenges they were facing. (An outline of the Household Covenant is provided in Appendix 1.)

Initially, I hoped I could develop a simple Bible study guide that could be broadly distributed and used by any group. This I did do, however, as I ran studies for a multitude of groups over a number of years, I began to understand that, while the prompts and suggestions in a Bible study resource were enough for some people to go on with, many others needed more than that. In particular, the task of critically analysing the normal practice in a given area, such as savings and investment, requires a certain amount of prior information and critical thinking. I also found that for a number of people, the habits of reading the Bible with a purely spiritualised lens meant they needed a bit of help to recognise the gritty social and economic issues it also addresses. While I found my own role in facilitating such thinking immensely rewarding, I quickly realised I could only ever do this with a limited number of people within a limited geographic area.

---

1 See www.mannagum.org.au

Thus I realised some time ago that what was needed was a book which provided the sort of information and thinking inherent in these Bible studies. It has been a bit longer coming than I had hoped, but this book is the result.

It is important for me to acknowledge that the thinking underpinning this book is rooted in a shared journey with a community of people. At the core of this community is the more than 20-year partnership that my wife, Kim, and I have shared in trying to live out our faith in our economic lives. Kim's skills, resolve and courage are central to the unfolding discoveries of our journey in this area. Beyond that, there have been countless conversations and exchanges of information, advice and books that have taken place with friends in Footscray, Cudgee, Bendigo and within the Common Rule that contribute a very large part of the background of this book and a substantial part of the concrete examples cited within. These conversations have ranged from the deeply theological to the detailed and practical ('Who is a good green energy provider?'; 'Is there a brand of washing machine that is fully recyclable?'), and they have shared a common inspiration in the Bible studies led by Peter Chapman.

I would like thank Kim, Simon Holt and Peter Chapman who have read and commented on earlier versions or parts of this text. A big thanks goes to Colin Taylor for the meticulous proofreading that he has undertaken with this text and many of my Manna Gum publications. Also, thanks to Beth Heron for her keen proof reading eye. And finally, I would like to thank all those who participated in Household Covenant Bible studies, the conversations from which have shaped this work.

The problem of normal life

Not so long ago, a team of Martian anthropologists came to Earth to continue their long-running, but very discreet, project of studying the apex species of their near-planetary neighbour. As tends to happen in the Martian academic sector, there comes a time when everything important seems to have been studied inside-out, so that young Martian academics, in order to find a niche, are forced into increasingly obscure areas of research. So it was that a couple of aspiring young alien visitors took up the extremely obscure topic of studying a sub-group called 'Christians' in the land mass known as 'Australia'. In particular, these researchers wanted to know in what ways this sub-group was different from the rest of the population.

What did these ingenious Martian inquirers uncover? As anthropologists, they were particularly interested in material culture and, as complete outsiders, they began with the very basics: food, housing, transport, wealth, employment, leisure time, etc. In what ways did this Christian sub-group differ from the mainstream culture?

Distressingly, they initially found very little that distinguished this group at all. Their daily habits of work, consumption and leisure seemed virtually identical to everyone else. Christians generally aspired to the same sorts of large, cooled and heated housing; they spent large amounts of money on impressive TVs to which they devoted many hours of serious study; they avidly consumed and upgraded new communications technology to which they devoted perhaps even more time; they made high use of the private automobile; and they tended to over-consume food which they knew to be ill-matched to their biology. The Martians also noticed that Christians tended to suffer from the same sort of malaises as the rest of the population, whether physical, social or mental. While there were some small differences in rates of marriage breakdown, depression or ill health due to 'lifestyle diseases' (obesity, diabetes, cardiovascular health), these were not statistically significant. They did notice that Christians tended to be grouped largely from the middle classes of society, they tended to have higher rates of tertiary education and they tended to vote for political groups which humans described as 'conservative'. However, so did many others – this was hardly a distinguishing feature.

Digging a little deeper, they began to notice some subtle differences from the rest of the population. Most significant of these was the fact that Christians attended a group meeting, on average between once a week and once a fortnight, usually on Sundays, and they tended also to commit some financial resources to the ongoing functioning of this gathering. This seemed to be the prime identifying characteristic of Christians in Australia. There were a few other differences: Christians tended to do more voluntary service in the community, they tended not to use smoked narcotics and they tended to consume less imbibed narcotics (though more than they let on). They also made less public use of linguistic devices known as 'expletives'. Finally, the Martians noticed that Christians were more likely to restrain their sexual activity to one partner, although, again, perhaps less than they let on.

On the whole, our alien observers came to the conclusion that being a Christian was equivalent to belonging to a sports club. It involved a certain level of time commitment and financial obligation, and it tended to influence language, the consumption of narcotics and who people slept with, all of which tended to be true of sports clubs. Just like belonging to a sports club, being a Christian in Australia seemed to be yet another optional layer that one could add to the base of what seemed a largely non-negotiable material culture.

What do we make of these observations of the Australian Christian? To be sure, their conclusions are not fair. There is much which our Martian anthropologists have failed to observe and perhaps even more below the surface which they could not possibly see. Nevertheless, as external observers without any preconceived ideas, is there anything to be learned from them?

There is one area where many human anthropologists, sociologists, social psychologists and even theologians would agree with our Martian observers. If you want to discover what a group of people is really on about, what their core beliefs are, then you do not focus on what they say but what they do. We live our lives according to our most deeply held beliefs and convictions, irrespective of whether they match up to our *articulated* beliefs and convictions. But if this is true, what is the significance of the fact that in 90 per cent of their lives Christians largely take their lead from mainstream culture? Does this mean that Christians basically hold 90 per cent of the same core convictions and beliefs as the mainstream culture, differing only on the margins?

This is a critical question for two very important reasons. The first is that, in Australia, as in the rest of the Western world, Christian belief is in crisis. Whether we are looking at the numerical decline of certain denominations, the rarity of conversions, the low rates of children following in the faith of their parents or the uncertainty of so many who remain in the pews (or the pulpit!), it seems clear that the dominant version of Christian faith is no longer cutting it. In so many ways, Christianity just seems to be irrelevant to the existential, ethical and lifestyle challenges that confront us from every angle.

The question of how we live and what we believe is a pressing one for another reason. If we say that, in 90 per cent of their lives, Christians basically live according to mainstream culture, then we are acknowledging a massive moral problem. It has been evident for some time that 'normal life', according to the model of Western consumer society, has become untenable. Indeed, there are three big generalisations we can make about our way of life:

1. The way we live cannot be sustained by the planet.
2. The way we live perpetuates global structures of injustice and inequality.
3. The way we live is no good for us either.

I will not trouble you with evidence for these statements here, as the rest of this book is filled with it. Most people reading this will probably already know something about climate change, or species extinction, or global inequality, or labour conditions in the developing world, or family breakdown, or the mental health epidemic. Most people reading this probably already know *something* of the truth of each of these statements, even if they have not been considered in such bleak terms or taken altogether. It turns out that, somehow, faith in Christ has not prevented us from being implicated in a destructive and idolatrous economic system.

Put together, all this can be overwhelming, and the instinctive response is either towards denial or paralysis. Can we find a way to live with such a stark assessment of our predicament and yet still move forward in hope?

Coming back to earth

In my previous book, *Coming Back to Earth*, I suggested that the seeming *thinness* of modern Christianity in the face of the massive challenges facing humanity is, in large part, a product of the privatisation and over-spiritualisation of faith. Over the last few centuries, the dominant understanding of Christian faith has been one that has been largely abstracted from the world of money, work, consumption and nature. Instead, the message of the Bible has been assumed to be one that is primarily concerned with the interior state of one's soul and its final destination after death: pie in the sky when you die. And thus, precisely during those centuries when Europe was undergoing an economic revolution that transformed social relations within countries, economic relations between countries, and the nature of humanity's exploitative relationship with the earth, Christians were, on the whole (though there has always been a counter-trend), losing the insight that their faith had anything to say about it all. Commerce, politics and economics were spheres where Christian faith had little to contribute other than the injunction to be upright, honest and to work hard at what you did.

Through the 19th and 20th centuries, Western civilisation drove the development of a world economy that was predicated on economic exploitation and ecological destruction, and that, in turn, came to drive a culture of mindless and frenetic consumerism. All of this largely happened with the tacit, and sometimes explicit, blessing of the church. Now, at the beginning of the 21st century, we are waking up to a nightmare in which life in the affluent West (even for many Christians) is confusing, conflicted and vacuous, in which global economic inequality is becoming ever more serious, and all this on a planet in the midst of an ecological crisis. No wonder so many are finding the platitudes of polite Christianity a little hard to swallow. We might say that Christianity in the West has had its head in the clouds and now it is being brought back to earth with something of a thud.

Does this mean that Christianity has proved to be fundamentally flawed and should be dispensed with? On the contrary, as GK Chesterton once said: 'The Christian ideal has not been tried and found wanting; it has been found difficult and left untried.' If we open the pages of the Bible, we find that it consistently and powerfully warns that the failure to observe limits in economic life results in the fracturing of society and creation and alienation from God. The concern is not just that our economic conduct in the world be ethical and just (although it is certainly that); rather, there is a deeper recognition that our economic lives reveal our deep allegiances. Most fundamentally, our economic lives reveal who or what we really worship. Thus, we find that in both the Old Testament and New, discussion of economic behaviour is frequently coupled with discussion of idolatry. Underpinning all of this is a fundamental principle that runs through the whole Bible: the material world and the spiritual world are not separate and independent realms; rather, they are inextricably intertwined. Spiritual movements have material consequences, whether good or bad, and material movements have spiritual consequences, whether good or bad.

At the foundation of the Christian gospel is the conviction that God's Word to humanity – the thing that God has to say to us – has become flesh in the person of Jesus of Nazareth. That is, the thing that God wanted to say to humanity could not just be accomplished by a voice from heaven or words on a page; it required a *whole life* to say it, from birth to death to resurrection. And that is because the gospel – literally the *good news* – concerns our *whole lives*, both spiritual and material.

More than that, we are told that Jesus came to us because God so *loved the world* – and the Greek word used for 'world' (*kosmos*) means the whole created order. We are told that, through Jesus, God is reconciling the whole *kosmos* back to himself. The foundation of the Lord's Prayer and the thing that Jesus' life embodied was 'Your kingdom come, your will be done, *on earth as in heaven*'. Indeed, the ultimate hope of the New Testament is not that human souls will finally attain 'heaven' after death, but that we will enjoy resurrected life on a restored earth, in which heaven is fully present. And at the heart of all this is the invitation to enter into *fullness of life* – 'the life that really is life' – which means to enter into the communion of love between God, humanity and creation.

This basic perspective is critical to maintain. When we encounter the Bible's various teachings on material and economic life, we need to understand that they are not simply ethical hoops for us to jump through to make us good and just; rather, they are fundamentally concerned with our participation in the communion of love, which is salvation and life itself. When we come back to earth, we find this is the place where God has been waiting for us to join him all along.

In *Coming Back to Earth*, I suggested that what the world needs of us and what is best for us are the same thing. And right now, the health of the world and the health of our souls require that we somehow begin to make a break with the culture of consumer gratification that has reared us and shaped us. As Paul puts it, we need to 'conform no longer to the pattern of this present world' (Rom 12:2 REB), and to do this requires a re-ordering of our household economies.

Coming home

In my first year of high school in the 1980s, Home Economics ('Home Ec') was a compulsory subject that everyone did for one semester. It included making a macramé owl, sewing a pencil case, cooking a meal (chicken chow mein) and baking a cake (chocolate). It was what was known amongst the students as 'a bludge subject'. As a fairly chauvinistic young male with an academic bent, Home Ec was a subject I held in low esteem, along with the girls (and it was only girls) who went on to choose it as an elective in the following years. (It didn't help that my chocolate cake, about which I was secretly quite excited, completely failed.) So there is not a small amount of irony in the fact that I have now come to the conclusion that home economics is central to the reconciling of economics and ecology that lies at the heart of humanity's great challenge in the 21st century. More than that, I have come to the conclusion that reclaiming a Christ-centred practice of home economics is central to our own spiritual health and to our witness in the world.

The Greek word for 'house', *oikos*, is the root word from which we get economics (*oikonomia*), ecology (*oikologia*) and ecumenical (*oikumene*). Economics describes the management and ordering of the work, consumption and finances of a household. Although economics as a discipline has now been abstracted to describe how we manage our affairs at the national and global levels, individual households still form the base unit of analysis. Ecology describes our attempts to understand the great household of nature and, in particular, to understand the interdependent relationships that support the functioning of that household. We have tended to think of economics and ecology as two separate spheres, when in fact the human economy exists entirely within the great household of nature and still depends entirely upon it, even if modern urban life gives us the illusion that we are somehow independent of nature. Ecumenism describes the movement towards unity within the household of God, usually referred to as 'the church'. It is based on the recognition that belonging to Christ draws us so deeply into relationship with others that we are members of a single body.

Generally, this last 'household', the church, is seen as having little to do with the other two. Moreover, in practice, the church even tends to have little to do with the ways in which its members run their homes. However, if we accept, as the Apostle Paul tells us, that faith in Christ requires presenting our 'bodies as living sacrifices' – that is, conforming our day-to-day bodily and material existence to the way of Jesus – then we must understand our individual households as not only the base of our participation in economy and ecology, but also the core site in which we enact or deny our membership in the household of faith in the hundreds of choices we make every day.

What's more, if we understand the household of faith as merely the first-fruits of the great reconciliation that God intends for the whole created order, but is yet to be accomplished, then a fuller understanding of the household of God should expand to encompass the whole household of nature, the human economy that exists within that and our own individual households within that. Thus, rather than a group of independent spheres, we have a picture of a series of concentric circles that comes down to our own homes. The question is, when we ask what it is at the centre of *that* circle, will we find Christ there?

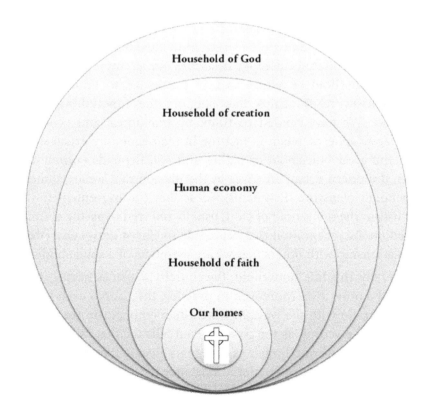

The purpose of this book is to provide a tool for Christian households seeking to live more responsibly, but its greater purpose is really to help us *live well*, and that requires the presence of Christ. For this reason, this book addresses seven areas of our day-to-day lives from which we generally have kept God out: our practice of hospitality, our work and leisure, our consumption, our relationship to nature, our financial giving, and our lending and borrowing of money. These seven areas of household economics may not give exhaustive coverage of our material lives, but they cover most of it.

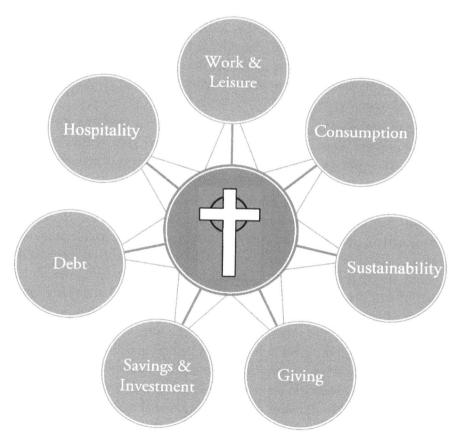

The aim of this book is to try to stop seeing these seven areas through the lens of 'normal life' and to try to see them through a *biblical* lens. The first step in this process is to simply ask the question, 'What's the problem in this area of life?' Jesus' proclamation of the kingdom of God began with a call to *repent* (e.g. Mt 4:17). The Greek word for repentance, *metanoia*, means to take on a new mind and a new way of seeing the world. Whereas repentance has often been misunderstood as simply an attitude of self-condemnation and guilt, it is more fully an exercise in seeing clearly. How we see the world determines how we live in it – Jesus' call to repentance is therefore a call to throw off the lens of normal life and take another look. In each of the seven areas of household economics, we will consider the ways in which the normal, received practice of these areas reflects deep seams of brokenness and disconnection, resulting in negative impacts upon our neighbours, the earth and ourselves.

The second step of the process is to ask, 'What does the Bible say on this matter?' One of the fundamental affirmations of this book is that the Bible not only has a great deal to say about our material lives, but that this teaching is *integral* to the whole message – to subtract the message concerning our material lives is not to have understood the biblical message. This does not mean the Bible always has clear and simple instructions that are easily translatable into modern life. Anyone who has spent time studying the Bible knows it is not an easy book to read and that how we use different bits of the Bible requires some wisdom and discernment. When we read in Exodus that anyone who profanes the Sabbath shall be put to death, we generally acknowledge that a literal reading of this text would not be wise or helpful! Much of our wrestling with the Bible involves trying to get beneath the packaging of ancient circumstances, language and customs the text is clothed in, to try find the *principle* at stake. If we then begin to find this principle being re-affirmed in different forms throughout the Bible, we know we have something that deserves serious consideration.

The third step of this process is then to ask, 'How can this be applied today?' Once again, applying principles we derive from the Bible to life within a mind-bogglingly complex global economy is not easy or straightforward. Many of the major challenges of modern living could never have been conceived in biblical times. Back then, the idea of 'fair trade' applied to face-to-face transactions and could never have envisaged a global supply chain with multiple layers of abstraction and removal. The Old Testament strictures around credit and interest on loans could never be applied in a global economy founded on debt. The challenge for us is always to move beyond trying to identify rules to follow and instead try to get at the heart of the matter to apply biblical discernment intelligently, creatively and realistically to the circumstances we find thrown at us. It requires information, wisdom and discernment and, even then, the question of what we ought to do is not always clear. The purpose of this book is not to provide definitive answers for how we must live, but rather to begin the process of fleshing out the challenges and possible responses.

The following chapters follow this three-fold process – asking, 'What is the problem?', 'What does the Bible say?', and 'How can we apply this today? – in each of the seven areas of household economics. At the end of each chapter, I provide a list of concrete examples of steps people have taken in an effort to translate Christ into that area of household economy. I have included these because I have come to understand that while some people readily translate concepts into practice, others need to get down to the nitty-gritty to make sense of something. It must be emphasised, however, that these are *examples* and not *benchmarks* by which to measure oneself. Neither should they be considered as the right or moral thing to do; rather, they are all provisional undertakings made by some people based on the information available and made within the context of a particular set of life circumstances. The most appropriate step for your household may well not have been considered within these pages.

The process of making changes can be fraught: some become paralysed from the perceived enormity of the challenge, while others leap in too quickly, taking on too much. In the first appendix, I outline a simple tool for change – the Household Covenant – that provides a framework for setting goals. It can be used by anyone, whatever his or her circumstances. Whether you directly use the Household Covenant process or just take on some of the ideas, the critical insight of this tool is that the most important part is not what changes we actually achieve – what we can 'achieve' is so dependent on our particular life circumstances – but rather lies simply in beginning to opening up these areas of life to God, allowing our spiritual lives to fill out our material lives, allowing Word to become flesh.

Perhaps one of the hardest spiritual challenges of this process comes when we see (as we inevitably must) how big the gap is between our own lives and the principles the Bible is calling us to live by. Opening up a biblical lens on life is painful and this can instinctively lead us to want to put away such a lens; but it is fundamentally this pain that God wants to open up in our lives, because it is the pain of reality. This is the place we must all come to, because it is only from here that God's healing and God's new possibilities begin:

Blessed are the poor in spirit, for they shall inherit the kingdom of heaven
(Mt 5:3).

This is the beginning of hope and abundant life; the beginning of an exciting new challenge and creative purpose to life.

A note on works, legalism and purity codes

There are a number of dangers in writing a book like this and they are all the old dangers that have continually beset biblical faith throughout history.

Most of the difficulties of the material discussed in this book stem from the fact that it invariably gets framed as 'ethics': the ways in which we conduct ourselves and regulate our behaviour in the world. As we have seen, this is a fundamental concern of the Bible from beginning to end. But the biblical story, and human history since, also amply testifies that there are a multitude of ways in which a focus on ethical conduct can lead us astray. As Chesterton once said, 'there are an infinity of angles at which one falls; only one at which one stands.' Therefore, if we are to embark on a rigorous ethical re-ordering of our material lives, it is critical we do so within as holistic a framework as possible.

The first difficulty of focusing on ethical conduct is perhaps the key reason, superficially at least, that so many Protestants have rejected such a task: that is, the danger of lapsing into a version of salvation by works. Perhaps because of some deep reasons of human psychology, human religion seems to have a predilection for assuming that we must somehow earn God's favour. Now, when put like this, most Christians would unhesitatingly affirm that our salvation (God's favour of us) is entirely an act of grace alone. We cannot earn it. And yet it is amazing that despite such an intellectual assent, there are thousands of different ways in which we can begin subconsciously to assume that certain actions are required of us to maintain God's favour. If, as we will do in this book, we begin to identify ethical problems with certain actions, and then begin to identify ways of behaving which seem better, it is very easy subconsciously to begin framing these things as 'right' and 'wrong' behaviours and, naturally, doing the 'wrong' thing will put us out of God's favour. Of course, we rarely consciously have this mental conversation with ourselves – it takes place in very subtle ways – but it is indeed a real danger.

There are a number of problems with this and the fact that it is 'bad theology' is the least of them. The major problem is that the motivating force behind our actions becomes a type of anxiety to please a grumpy God rather than the motivation of love. There is indeed a very real connection between our ethical behaviour and our salvation, but it is not that of cause and effect; ethical conduct cannot 'earn' salvation. Rather, the re-ordering of our lives by 'ethical' standards is the natural outworking of what happens when 'God's love has been poured into our hearts' (Rom 5:5). We do not earn salvation by the conduct of our lives, but rather *salvation takes shape in the conduct of our lives*.

Another problem with beginning to frame ethical challenges into simplistic categories of 'right' and 'wrong' is that many of the challenges we face are fiendishly complex and trying to determine what is a better course of action usually requires two things: (i) lots of good information; and (ii) some sort of subjective judgement. The reality is that there are many grey areas. In this context, it's virtually impossible that we will get everything 'right', if there is such a thing. Moreover, there are so many different fronts to work on at once that, if we were required to 'be in the right' all the time, most of us would simply find it an impossible standard to achieve. The great point of the gospel message is that we do not need to try to *justify* ourselves by the conduct of our lives, but rather we are simply called to follow Jesus in loving the world, as best we can. 'Love covers a multitude of sins' (1 Pet 4:8).

Such an understanding liberates us from that great tyranny of needing our whole lives to match up to the same consistent ethical standard. Cynics will often try to undermine efforts at ethical action by pointing out that one's efforts in one area are inconsistent with one's behaviour in another area. The implication is that the failure to achieve ethical consistency in all areas of life at once invalidates ethical efforts in *any* area. This is a line of thinking that is perfectly suited to doing nothing and accepting the status quo. Moreover, in the complex world in which live, complete consistency is impossible. We should certainly desire and strive for as much consistency as we can, but while such a desire can be a good servant to our efforts, it is a bad master. Let us instead try as best we might, accepting that there will always be some sort of shortcomings to our best efforts. Such a recognition continually brings us back to our recognition of our need of God: 'Blessed are the poor in spirit'.

Another danger in focusing on ethical conduct is one that formed a major tension between Jesus and the Pharisees: that is, the continual tendency of humans to turn guiding principles into arbitrary laws. Once a legalistic view of 'right' and 'wrong' begins to develop, it is inevitable that it will then be used to determine *who* is in the right and who is in the wrong. Of course, determining who is right and who is wrong is really a way of saying who is 'in' and who is 'out'; it leads to an exclusive community of the elect that has little tolerance or ability to relate to 'sinners' and 'the unclean' – in effect, a community of the self-righteous. That is not the way of the gospel. The great struggle of Jesus and Paul, and the one that created so much opposition, was to call into being a community of grace whose core understanding was that it was a community of sinners in need of the new life that comes from God.

A related concern is that the underlying motivation for following codes of ethical conduct can subtly transmute from a desire to do what is right into a desire to be free from any taint of sin or, even worse, to be *seen* to be free from any such taint. That is, in religious terms, an ethical code can easily become a purity code. Here, the concern has shifted from being about the other to a concern about self and, once again, this can be a powerful force towards exclusive community.

Herein lies the difficulty. The nature of daily life is such that we cannot undergo a process of spiritual discernment every time we need to make a decision that has some sort of ethical implications. We need to have an ethical framework or codes of conduct that, in effect, do this for us. Certainly, there is a fair bit of work and discernment in establishing such a framework in our lives, but once in place it can do the heavy lifting of day-to-day decision making. Without such frameworks where we have already done a substantial amount of ethical and biblical reflection, we are all at sea in a powerful and persuasive consumer culture that is incessantly making demands of us.

Our great need is to develop ethical frameworks for living that are robust enough to guide us through the challenges of modern life, but ones we can hold lightly enough so that they do not become a measure of righteousness and purity we apply either to ourselves or to others. There is no easy way of doing this other than to be continually alert to the symptoms: do we worry about our standing with God based on our various choices; do we worry about how others see us; do we look down on those who don't match our own ethical standards? This means we need to have a decent introspective awareness about the sources of our motivations. The same ethical code of conduct can be either a life-giving guide or a soul-destroying legalism – it all depends on why and how we use it.

There is one final danger. The focus of this book is to counteract the ways in which Christian faith has been over-spiritualised, neglecting the significance of material life. However, there is a danger that we may go too far in this and make the gospel entirely about material matters, where everything is always about politics and economics, to the neglect of the profound personal and spiritual message of the gospel. Our great need is to always hold these two things – spiritual life and material life – together. Ultimately, we must be careful that focusing on ethics and our material lives does not become a substitute for the real thing: faith in Christ that is founded on a real, personal and ongoing engagement with Him.

A personal note

This book is not a work of abstract thought, but rather is directly rooted in the practice of household economy that Kim (my wife) and I have worked at over the last two decades. This is both its strength and its weakness. The strength is that it is grounded in the complexity and necessary compromises of our real experience. I know that the sorts of life movements discussed in this book are *attainable* because, by and large, we and others have been living by them. The weakness is that this book will inevitably reflect our own biases and compromises. Perhaps, for reasons of circumstance, we have been able to go further in some areas than is reasonable to expect others to do. Perhaps (indeed I am sure of it) we have compromised and not gone nearly far enough in others.

Even so, this last weakness is, perversely, also a strength, for one of the 'virtues' of our story is that we have been far from heroic in making life changes. There is nothing in our life story that even remotely compares to the self-denial or sacrifices of a Dorothy Day or Shane Claiborne. I have drawn much inspiration from people like these, but sometimes their example can serve to de-motivate those of us who are more timid. By comparison, our story has been rather ordinary. Nevertheless, by a process of conscientiously and consistently taking small steps over a 20-year period we find our economic lives now differ quite markedly from the Australian norm.

Despite being in the lowest income quintile for Australian households, we are able to give away at least 12 per cent of our income each year; and yet our experience of finances is one of abundance and security. Our household energy consumption is well under half the comparable average and most of it is being supplied by our rooftop solar panels. We send only one shopping bag of waste to landfill each week and nearly all of our organic waste (except our poo) is processed on-site. Neither Kim nor I own a personal mobile phone, although Kim has one for her work. We have one TV in our house and it is second-hand. Indeed, much of our clothing, household furniture and electrical goods are second-hand. Kim and I both work part-time and so are able to contribute volunteer time in the community during the week, on top of our involvement in our local church. Our children (11 and 13 at the time of writing) have a fraction of the clothes, toys, junk food and access to electronic devices their peers do, and yet their lives are rich in relationships and experiences. Beyond these visible differences, perhaps our major testimony is that investing time, thought, energy and creativity into our household economy - its work, rest and consumption - has been profoundly rich and rewarding. To be sure, our lives are characterised by many of the strains, conflicts, tensions and conundrums that beset most Australian families; however, beneath that is a firm foundation of meaning and purpose.

Even so, our general week-to-week experience *feels* like a fairly normal middle-class Australian existence; comfortable, secure and not very challenging. And that is because our current life position is not the product of any massive leap of faith, but of a series of consistent choices.

Perhaps most important have been the paths we have avoided - going backwards is always much harder than taking new steps forward.

Of course, a limitation in writing this book from a base of personal experience is that real-life stories are grounded in particular contexts and the contexts of different households vary so dramatically. The boundaries of what is possible or wise depend so much on the mix of life circumstances that surround us; life stage, family context, education, employment status and possibilities, housing, geographic location, health and the list goes on. Movements that are relatively easy for a young couple with no children may be beyond imagining for a family with teenage kids and a mortgage. On the other hand, we need to be careful not to grant too much weight to context and use it as a cop-out that essentially enslaves us in the stream of 'circumstance'. For this reason, although this book is essentially rooted in our own experience, I have not written it from a first person perspective (except this bit!) but have tried to write it from a broader perspective that incorporates the practices and examples of a range of other people. Almost every possibility discussed in this book is being practised by someone who is otherwise fairly ordinary.

My prayer is that you will find this book useful as a prompt and a guide. It cannot be a prescription for how you must live - that is between you and God.

SEVEN AREAS OF HOUSEHOLD ECONOMY

1. HOSPITALITY
Opening our homes

The central concern of this book is whether our homes are open to the transformative work of God in Christ. We have been deeply shaped by our culture to think of our homes as 'our space': a place in which we shut out the world to attend to ourselves, whether that be through rest, amusement, indulgence or licking our wounds. But what if the very thing we need, the thing that is good for us and that heals us, is a deeper, fuller and more substantive relationship to God, and through God, to the rest of the world? In many ways, the ancient Christian understanding of hospitality - the act of welcoming the stranger into our homes - is a motif that captures the concerns of the following chapters. How can our homes reflect a more generous embrace of 'the other', whether it is God, our neighbours near and far or creation itself? And, of course, the place to start is to explore how our homes can be more open to our immediate human neighbours, especially those who are not welcome elsewhere.

What's the Problem?

In recent times, there has been an upsurge of interest and TV programs centred around 'the good life'. In particular, there has been something of a gastronomic revolution, with reality TV cooking programs leading the charge in bringing fine dining to a mass audience. Undoubtedly, there have been some positive elements to this, such as Jamie Oliver's campaign to get families to return to eating home-cooked meals together around a table. However, by far the greater emphasis of this burgeoning industry is on pushing food as the new frontier in consumer gratification - what some are calling 'food porn'. What has been little noted, though, is how this new culture of gratification influences how we think about hospitality, making it almost indistinguishable from entertainment.

To a large extent, 'hospitality' in our culture is a practice of nurturing our social circle: whether that be friends, professional colleagues or even visiting notables. Of course, there is nothing wrong with any of these; sharing a meal with people is a great way of deepening relationships and mutual understanding. The problem starts to become apparent when we begin to ask who gets into our social circle and who does not. In a modern, highly urbanised, individualised society, our social lives are channelled to be with people who are basically like ourselves. This happens partly as a result of our choices: for most people, both their work and their leisure activities will tend to funnel them towards those who have similar interests and similar socio-economic status. But it also occurs, to a very large degree, because of the social geography of our lives: modern cities tend to group us in large zones, sometimes whole suburbs, according to housing cost and quality, which, to an unprecedented degree, only contain people of a roughly similar socio-economic status. Whether by choice or not, the hard wiring of our weekly lives tends to mean that we have very limited encounters with 'the stranger' - those who are not like us.

This has a number of implications. Perhaps the greatest of these, from a Christian perspective, is simply the *social distance* this places between those of us in the middle-class mainstream and those who are more marginal in society. To the extent that the church is now largely a middle-class institution, this means there is a social distance between the church and those for whom it espouses a special care and concern. Not only does this place a large practical obstacle in the way of churches reaching out to the disadvantaged - how do you reach those with whom you have no contact? - it can also have a negative impact on the actions of churches when they do attempt to reach out.

Throughout history, and especially in the last couple of hundred years, churches have sometimes done more harm than good when they have tried in some way to reach out to 'the poor' without having much idea of how 'the poor' experience their poverty. That is, too often we seek to ameliorate poverty, or even worse, to *solve* poverty, without really understanding what 'poverty' is. Whether that was some of the patronising ways churches sought to evangelise the urban poor during the Industrial Revolution; or the ways that churches in Australia sought to address indigenous disadvantage by breaking up families and suppressing culture; or the more recent fad for churches to build orphanages in countries like Cambodia or the Philippines; again and again, good intentions have done harm when they have not been matched by a sympathetic and deep understanding that is rooted in experience of the real circumstances of those we call 'the poor'.

While the language of 'the poor' certainly occupies an important place in the Bible (as we will see), a simplistic application of this language to our own times can mean we sometimes fail to notice the massive differences in experiences amongst those who are in some way disadvantaged. There are radical differences between the experiences and needs of newly arrived refugees, the long-term unemployed and welfare-dependent who are struggling with multiple addictions, and the isolated disabled or aged pensioner. Moreover, when we compare these to the experiences of a farmer in Malawi or a textile worker in Bangladesh, then we begin to see that any simplistic idea of what it is to be 'poor' is clearly inadequate.

While some financial hardship is often common to many who are 'disadvantaged' in Australia, a comparison with the experience of some in much poorer countries helps us see that *material want* is not necessarily the most important or central dimension of their experience. Rather, it is the experience of *social marginalisation* - of not belonging - that is often the dimension of 'poverty' most central to the diverse groups of 'the poor' in our own country. Whether it be for reasons of language and culture, economic redundancy (that is, not being needed in our economy), long-term family dysfunction or physical or intellectual ability, the feeling of not belonging can be particularly sharp in the midst of a culture of busy, affluent, independent, capable, consumer individuals. Social distance is not just a barrier to making contact with the marginalised, it is in fact central to the experience of marginalisation.

The experience of marginalisation is often reinforced by many of the structures we have erected to help the disadvantaged. As welfare services have become larger, more professionalised and more bureaucratic, they increasingly tend to treat people as categories and have less and less ability to respond to them as human beings. While the services provided may be necessary and helpful, they can simultaneously be degrading and disempowering. In simple terms, it is very hard for a large institution to be *hospitable* in a way that provides a sense of welcome and affirmation.

What Does the Bible Say?

In one sense, the Bible, as a whole, is a story about hospitality: it is a story about how we, who had become strangers to God, have nevertheless received a gracious and open welcome into God's household:

> So he came and proclaimed peace to you who were far off and peace to those who were near; for through him both of us have access in one Spirit to the Father. So then you are no longer strangers and aliens, but you are citizens with the saints and also members of the household of God ... (Eph 2:17-19)

This reaching out to those who are 'far off' is part of the essence of God that the Bible reveals to us; as such, it is also part of the essence of *who God calls us to be* in this world: 'be imitators of God' (Eph 5:1). Abraham and Sarah, the spiritual ancestors of God's people in the world, are characterised as exemplars of hospitality. In Genesis 18 (vv.1-15), they unhesitatingly go out of their way to provide a warm and generous welcome to three strangers, *inviting them in* to their camp and *honouring them* with food and attention. It is in the practice of their hospitality that Abraham and Sarah received the blessing for which they yearned but dared not to hope for. Immediately following this story, Lot's welcome of two of the strangers, now disclosed to us as angels, is contrasted with the Sodomite's hostility towards them and it is his welcome of the strangers that saves Lot and his family from the destruction of the city. According to the prophet Ezekiel, Sodom's guilt lay in the fact that it had 'abundant food, and careless ease, but she did not help the poor and needy' (Ezek 16:49); that is, Sodom's guilt lay in a failure of hospitality.

The Books of the Law - the Torah - are full of injunctions for the Israelites to be a society that is hospitable to the stranger and alien in their midst. Recognising the inherent vulnerability of strangers, the command 'You shall not wrong or oppress a resident alien' is repeated continually throughout the books of the Law. More than that, Leviticus and Deuteronomy go on to insist that 'you shall *love* the alien as yourself' (Lev 19:34, Deut 10:19). The laws concerning the harvesting of fields and orchards give a very practical expression to this hospitality, requiring that with every harvest there be some left over, not only for the poor of their own people, but also for the vulnerable stranger in their midst (Lev 23:22, Deut 24:20-21). Again and again, God's people are being asked to treat the stranger as one of themselves, applying the same standards, care and justice to them as they would their brethren. Again and again, underlying their treatment of the stranger, the Israelites are called to *identify themselves with the stranger*: 'you know the heart of an alien, for you were aliens in the land of Egypt' (Ex 23:9).

Despite such commands, the development of cleanliness laws and food taboos within Judaism tended, over time, to harden the barriers between the socially acceptable and outsiders, whether they were 'sinners and tax collectors', the poor and unclean or foreigners. This is the background against which the example and teaching of Jesus is so startling. The question of who is offering hospitality and to whom it is being offered is central to the storyline of the gospels and if we miss this dynamic then we will miss the full force, scandal and beauty of the way of Jesus.

Throughout the gospel story, we continually find Jesus sharing meals with people. What is so striking about these meals is how social barriers to hospitality seem invisible to him. We find Jesus in the homes of the religiously upright (Simon the Pharisee), the homes of the working battler (Simon the fisherman), the homes of the ostracised (Levi the tax collector) and the homes of the corrupted super-rich (Zacchaeus). In most of these encounters, Jesus is in fact the *guest* - it is in inviting Jesus into their homes that people have some of the most important experiences of healing, conviction of sin and of salvation. And yet, though a guest, Jesus frequently seems to be playing the role of *host*; it is Jesus who seems to be welcoming in those present. His presence in the home of Simon the Pharisee is enough even to draw in a woman who was a notorious 'sinner' (perhaps a prostitute), something that was otherwise unimaginable (Lk 7:36-50).

What is unquestionable is that Jesus made a special point of mixing with the socially outcast, the poor, the sick, the tormented and the hurting. Whereas his religious contemporaries had become preoccupied with the fear of the infectiousness of 'sin' and 'impurity', Jesus shows that it is in fact *holiness* that is infectious. Wherever Jesus goes, his holiness - that is, his *wholeness* - rubs off on other people, bringing restoration and healing. Whether it was tax collectors, prostitutes, lepers, the bleeding woman or a Gentile, Jesus showed a graciousness of welcome where others would have been guarded or even hostile.

If the example of Jesus was not pointed enough, the importance of welcoming the stranger is driven home in his teaching. In Luke 14, Jesus (during a dinner party!) makes a direct challenge to the idea of hospitality as a means of nurturing one's social circle:

> When you give a luncheon or a dinner, do not invite your friends or your brothers or your relatives or rich neighbours, in case they may invite you in return, and you would be repaid. But when you give a banquet, invite the poor, the crippled, the lame and the blind. And you will be blessed, because they cannot repay you, for you will be repaid at the resurrection of the righteous. (Lk 14:12-14)

Directly following this teaching, Jesus goes on to tell a story that further underlines the centrality of welcoming in the marginal to the kingdom of God. In the Parable of the Great Banquet (Lk 14:15-24), Jesus tells of a great feast thrown by an expansive host. In this story, those who have independent means in society (lands, oxen, well-married), though invited, apparently feel they have little need to participate in the great feast and therefore absent themselves. In contrast, 'the poor, the crippled, the blind and the lame', and those wandering 'the roads and the lanes', are, in striking language, *compelled to come* to the banquet.

The forcefulness of the language is dramatically underscored in Matthew 25 in the teaching of the sheep and the goats (vv.31-46). Significantly, this is a teaching about judgement and it is the only such teaching in the gospels that has specific criteria attached to it. What are the criteria? Feeding the hungry, drink for the thirsty, welcoming the stranger, clothes for the naked, care for the sick and visiting those in prison. That is, *our hospitality to 'the least of these' is a fundamental signifier of our participation in the kingdom of God.*[1]

Indeed, there is a sense in the gospels that the hospitality we are called to practise is greater than our means to do so. In Mark's account of the feeding of the 5000, the disciples' concern for the welfare of the crowds leads them to suggest that Jesus should send them away so that they may buy something to eat for themselves (Mk 6:36). But Jesus responds: 'You give them something to eat'. It is in the midst of making their own limited means (five loaves and two fish) available in hospitality that a miracle occurs. The collection of *twelve* (the number of Israel) baskets of leftovers at end of the meal signifies that what is taking place in this shared meal is in fact the restoration of a fractured national community. And in case we might be tempted to interpret this narrowly as applying only to an in-group ('Israel'), the story of the feeding of the 4000 two chapters later ends with the collection of *seven* baskets of leftovers – the number of all creation (Mk 8:8). In both of these stories, a kind of healing is taking place in which boundaries are being overcome through the discovery of abundance when hospitality is offered, despite what initially seemed to be hopelessly inadequate means.

---

1 Some commentators have sought to use Jesus' reference to 'these least of these *my brethren*' (v.40) to suggest that this teaching applies only to our treatment of other Christians. However, as we have been seeing, such a narrow interpretation flies in the face of Jesus' own example of going beyond the bounds of the 'insiders' to continually and pointedly reach out to the 'outsiders'. In particular, through the Parable of the Good Samaritan (Lk 10:25-37,) Jesus expands the concept of loving one's neighbour to include an heretical enemy.

And if the example and direct teaching of Jesus were not enough, it is hard to overstate the importance of the fact that his death and resurrection are bracketed by shared meals. In Jesus' last supper with his disciples, the sharing of the most ordinary elements of the meal – bread and wine – comes to take on the cosmic significance of his self-giving sacrifice and it is this very basic shared meal that has come to form one of the most central and foundational practices of Christianity through the ages. Moreover, the fullest encounters with the resurrected Jesus also take place over shared meals. Significantly, for Cleopas and his friend, it is in the breaking of bread that the resurrected Jesus, who had been hidden to them, is made fully known (Lk 24:30-32).

It is not surprising, then, that one of the most distinctive and controversial aspects of early Christianity was its practice of shared meals. Acts (Ch. 10 and 11) gives an account how visionary experiences and an encounter with the Gentile centurion, Cornelius, led Peter to the scandalous conclusion that following Christ required abandoning Jewish food laws in favour of hospitality. But this was such a huge step for faithful Jews that even Peter, when put under pressure, felt it difficult to maintain at first (see Galatians 2:11-14). It took the courageous and controversial ministry of Paul to continuously and strenuously insist that the way of Jesus required a radical boundary-crossing hospitality in which there is neither Jew nor Gentile, slave nor free, male nor female, but instead one new humanity in Christ (Gal 3:28; Eph 2:15; Col 3:11). In Paul's letters to the churches in Corinth and Rome, it is clear that he sees their practice of shared meals as critical to their embodiment of faith in Christ, ensuring that the more well-to-do are considerate of the needs and feelings of poorer members (1 Cor 11:17-33). Paul understands that bringing people together across cultural and ethnic boundaries raises some complex issues in terms of the ethics of eating; but again and again his constant encouragement is that people be *hospitable of one another's differences* (see Rom 14:1-23 and 1 Cor 8:1-13; 10:1-33).[2]

---

2 I have written about this in greater length in *Coming Back to Earth*. See the final chapter: 'The Law of Love: Jesus, Paul and the Ethics of Eating'.

As a whole, the New Testament epistles continue to affirm the importance of hospitality to the Christian way of life. In Romans 12, Paul provides a condensed summary of the core practices of the Christian way of life – one of the great passages of the New Testament so it is not surprising that his list includes the exhortations to 'extend hospitality to strangers' and 'associate with the lowly' (Rom 12:13,16). The letter of James powerfully echoes the teaching of Jesus in condemning preference for the wealthy and neglect of the poor in hospitality (Jas 2:1-13). And finally, the letter to the Hebrews brings us full circle in recalling the example of Abraham and Sarah when exhorting: 'Do not neglect to show hospitality to strangers, for by doing that some have entertained angels without knowing it' (Heb 13:2).

In summary, we can see that the biblical approach to hospitality, especially that of the New Testament, contains three layers of concerns. Firstly, there is simply a concern about the *material needs* of the poor, the vulnerable and the stranger, and an admonition that both our households and our social institutions be hospitable to these needs. Secondly, there is a deep understanding of the role of shared meals and opening our homes in providing *social recognition* to those whom society is apt to ignore or to ostracise. In this sense, Jesus' practice of eating with people across social boundaries can be understood as part of his wider ministry of *healing*. Thirdly, there is an understanding that the way in which the followers of Jesus share meals together and with others, provides a profound *sign of the kingdom* that is being both proclaimed and anticipated.

How Might We Respond?

In other areas of household economics discussed in this book, we will be challenged to think about how our practices of household economy impact upon 'the poor'. In this area, the challenge is to think about how we *experience* 'the poor' and, particularly, what place they have in our homes and social lives. In the above discussion, we can see that a Christian practice of hospitality has three layers of concern to it: (i) to simply help meet someone's physical needs; (ii) to provide the social recognition of persons that we all need; and (iii) to provide a sign of the kingdom, however fleeting and ephemeral.

It is important to recognise that, for people who have been formed in a culture of individualism, in which our homes have been privatised and isolated from the lives of others and in which there is a great social distance between the marginal and the middle-class mainstream, the New Testament ethic of hospitality seems particularly threatening and demanding. Moreover, the depth of the dysfunctionality and brokenness found in some segments of society is deeply unsettling. There is little to be gained by demanding an heroic standard of hospitality that few can attain. The important thing is to make sure that our inability (for the time being, at least) to do some things does not prevent us from identifying steps *that we can take*. And perhaps the process to begin such a journey is not to think first about our own household practice, but rather to begin with practices and culture of the Christian communities to which we belong.

Communities of hospitality

Perhaps it is best not to think of hospitality as an individual virtue that we develop but rather *a culture in which we participate*. There is no doubt that some people do indeed seem to have a gift for hospitality, and there is much to be learned by observing such people, but we need to be careful that we do not simply abrogate the responsibility for hospitality to them. Individual acts of hospitality become much easier when they draw on a corporate practice and culture.

Throughout Christian history, there have been communities that have specialised in offering welcome to the stranger, from the early Benedictine and Celtic monasteries all the way through to modern groups such as the Catholic Worker movement, L'Arche and the Sanctuary Movement. In Australia, groups such as the Waiters Union in Brisbane and Urban Seed in Melbourne have tried to provide places of welcome for the mentally ill, homeless and drug-dependent. In most of these cases, meals and sometimes accommodation have been an important part of offering that welcome; however, the stress is not so much upon the service provided as on the human connection that takes place through it. And all of these exemplars of hospitality have recognised that they can only offer such service as a community where burdens are shared, encouragement provided, and prayers are offered.

The local church is a community and an institution that affords many opportunities for the corporate practice of hospitality. The Sunday service, the community ministries of local churches and the social services of the various denominations all provide sites in which we can encounter the stranger and which open opportunities to offer hospitality. Often, one need not even go outside the Christian community to find people on the margins, whether they are the aged, disabled, migrant, welfare-dependent or simply the lonely, awkward people who struggle to fit in. This is an important point to emphasise: before seeking to extend our hospitality in more challenging directions, we should first develop the *eyes to see* the stranger who is already in our midst. The foundation of a Christ-centred practice of hospitality is an empathetic sensitivity to those who are broken, hurting and vulnerable; those whom social groups (of any form) so unconsciously tend to exclude and marginalise.

To this end, it is worth thinking about the various gatherings of Christian communities as opportunities to practice hospitality in a space that is relatively 'safe' for both parties. While inviting someone into your home is perhaps the most profound form of social recognition, there are many cases where, initially at least, the differences in culture may make this quite an uncomfortable experience for all. The differences of language and culture of a newly arrived migrant or refugee family may actually be less of an obstacle than the cultural divide that exists between busy, educated middle-class Australians and those who are long-term unemployed and welfare-dependent. Judging what is appropriate takes some sensitivity to both the people and the context involved. Practising hospitality consistently in safe spaces allows the possibility that it may develop more naturally into offering hospitality from one's house.

The key task is to find ways to help people feel both *welcome* and *at home* within Christian gatherings. This need not only be a matter of your own personal practice of hospitality; if you can find people of similar concerns, it is something that is best talked about and practised together. Ideally, forming a culture of hospitality would be a concern of the whole congregation and a lens that informed the whole process of gathering, from worship through to cuppas afterwards.

Similarly, volunteering in a church outreach service or denominational welfare service can be a good way of taking a first step towards placing yourself outside your social comfort zone, amongst those who are not like you. Once again, such an environment often provides a structured and safe space for such encounters, where they otherwise might be too threatening. That said, it is important to be aware that the culture of such services can sometimes be dominated by a charity or welfare mindset that tends to work against hospitality and welcome. There can also be a wide degree of variability in the quality and culture of outreach and welfare services, so some discernment is needed. At their worst, charities and welfare agencies can even deepen the experience of alienation, even while providing a necessary service.

If volunteering in a social service, it is always good to be continually asking how interactions between people can be made more human. One of the learnings of Christian communities who have excelled in hospitality is that this is a discipline requiring reflective practise. While some people seem to have natural gifts in making others welcome, there are still skills to be developed and lessons that will need to be learned and this is best done amongst a community of people which can discern the path of wisdom prayerfully.

Opening our homes

Ultimately, hospitality involves sharing lives as opposed to providing a service, and this is most powerfully done through our homes. Moreover, unlike welfare, hospitality is often reciprocated: being hospitable sometimes mean being prepared to *receive* hospitality from others and going into their homes and lives.

Just as the best practices of Christian hospitality have been rooted in communities and institutions that nurture that practice, so, too, home-based hospitality (as opposed to 'entertaining') requires a structure of life that can make it possible. It does not take much reflection to realise that the most important dimension of this is *time*: in essence, hospitality is the giving of time. We cannot really think about the giving of hospitality separate from the structure of our time commitments – that is, the forms of our work and leisure. This is the subject of the next chapter, so we will not pursue it further here; but it is important to see hospitality as integrated into a broader approach of household economy. Like all the other areas of household economy, a Christian approach to hospitality requires a level of intentionality, mindfulness and discipline.

Nowhere is this more the case than in seeking to open our homes to people who do not naturally come into our social circle and especially to those who are in some way marginal. Generally, this requires some level of forethought and prior decision that helps us firstly to see opportunities to offer hospitality when they crop up and, secondly, to nudge us over the line in actually taking the step when the opportunity arises. Of course, if we are never in spaces where we are mixing with people who are not like us, then this will be almost impossible.

Once again, it is important to emphasise that some wisdom is needed here. One of the learnings that comes from communities who have excelled in hospitality is that maintaining a safe and welcoming space ultimately requires some limits and boundaries around who can be invited in and under what terms. There are behaviours and levels of dysfunctionality and brokenness that most homes simply cannot accommodate and that require the attention of people, communities and institutions with specific vocations and training. In particular, we need to be very careful about what sort of exposure to brokenness our children can healthily accommodate. While it is undoubtedly good for children to have a wide and rich social exposure, there are limits to this and these need to be discerned in relation to their age and particular needs and life circumstances. The problem is that we have come to draw these lines so narrowly that we confuse the awkward and uncomfortable with the threatening. And there is no way of getting around the fact that, however we might qualify the texts, Jesus is calling us to a practice of hospitality that leads us all out of our comfort zones.

It is helpful to reflect on what hospitality, at its best, does for people. As has been mentioned, at the heart of the best hospitality is not the ability to delight, impress or entertain, but the ability to make someone *feel at home*; to feel like there is a natural welcome and acceptance where social facades are no longer necessary. This suggests that the practice of hospitality may indeed sometimes be very different from entertaining people. Of course, there are no rules and context is everything, but generally speaking, gastronomic feats are not necessarily the most conducive way of deepening human connection. Sometimes, sharing the simplest of meals can signal to someone that they are truly welcome. Similarly, the physical appearance of a household is important, but not necessarily in the ways that we tend to think. In entertaining guests, the emphasis is often on achieving a spotless and sophisticated décor that boosts our social pegging. However, such an environment does not necessarily make people feel at home, especially if they are more socially marginal in some way. Not surprisingly, people will tend to feel at home in places that feel like a home; that is, places that feel they are being inhabited by real people rather than the representatives of a socially successful class.

In this sense, a deeper practice of hospitality is tied to a fuller investment of meaning and life into our homes and the relationships that form our homes. Thus, hospitality is intimately connected with the other dimensions of household economy discussed in this book. A key part of what is communicated through hospitality is not just the words spoken or the food and drink offered, but *the sort of home* into which people are invited. Homes that have been thoughtfully structured around the attempt to show love and care for the world will inevitably communicate something of this to those welcomed in, even if such things are never really mentioned. The importance of this sort of unspoken communication is not to be underestimated.

Examples of steps people have taken

- Commit to reading and discussing one or two of the works of Dorothy Day (e.g. *Loaves & Fishes* or *House of Hospitality*) or Henri Nouwen (e.g. *Compassion* or *The Wounded Healer*). This could be done as a couple or with others.
- Set aside one night a week when you share a meal with others.
- Identify one person or family who is lonely or on the margins of your church/community. Invite them over for a meal and begin to get to know each other.
- Find out about what local services or groups work with the aged or disabled. Can you help in any way?
- Volunteer at a local soup kitchen, shelter or clinic to find out about local needs.
- What are the needs of local refugee or migrant communities? Can you help?
- Undertake an exposure-type program with a community that excels in providing hospitality to those on the margins or sponsor a friend or family member to join one.

2. WORK & LEISURE
Sabbath-centred living

Broadly defined, work and leisure are what we spend most of our lives doing when we are not sleeping. It accounts for two-thirds of our time on this Earth, and almost all of the energy we expend while here. Time is the most valuable thing we have: it cannot be increased or replaced. How we choose to spend time is how we choose to live our lives. Time is the most valuable thing we can give to God and it is the most valuable thing we can give to other people. The choices we make about how we spend our time – that is, our choices about work and leisure – are the foundation of our economic behaviour and therefore, of our impact in the world.

What's the Problem?

One of the key characteristics of our modern condition is that so many of us are time-poor. The question 'Have you been busy?' is a standard part of our casual greetings to one another. For many, feeling stressed and guilty about not spending enough time with significant people is a perpetual condition.

The social effects of our time poverty are profound. There is little doubt that it plays a significant role in relationship breakdown leading to family breakdown and also to the increasing sense of alienation between parents and children. Time poverty is also a key ingredient in what has become known as community breakdown, which is the decline of participation in community clubs and associations such as sporting clubs, charities, churches and interest groups, and the decline in voluntary service. Social isolation and community breakdown are generally recognised as significant contributing factors in the rising incidence of mental illness in Australia, especially depression.

Time poverty is also an important determinant of our economic behaviour. Much of the structure of our consumer economy has developed around servicing people who are time-poor. Things such as 24-hour supermarkets, mobile phones, pre-made pasta sauce, dog walking services, ATMs, internet shopping and take-away food are all part of the burgeoning convenience economy that traps people in a cycle of dependence: they allow us to cope better with our lack of time, but require that we have higher incomes to be able to pay for all of these things. In turn, the higher our incomes the greater the demands that work tends to place on our time, therefore committing us to dependence on the convenience economy.

The convenience economy plays a large role in the overall destructiveness of our wider economy. Supermarkets, born in the US during the Great Depression, are the flagship of the convenience economy. They have become so ingrained in our way of life that it almost impossible to imagine living without them. In Australia, Woolworths and Coles control 75 per cent of food retail, giving them enormous power to dictate terms to growers and food manufacturers. The pressure that supermarkets place on farmers is a major factor driving unsustainable farming practices, such as overuse of chemicals and irrigation, exhaustion of soils, erosion and salinity. Similarly, the global reach of Western supermarkets has contributed to the undermining of poor smallholder farmers in developing countries, in favour of large-scale agribusiness. Supermarkets have encouraged excessive packaging of foods and are notorious for their vast wastefulness. It is estimated that perhaps as much as one-third of all food produced in the world goes to waste.

If supermarkets are the flagship of the convenience economy, then communications technology is the vanguard. Our consumption of all sorts of time-saving devices – especially telecommunications devices – now makes it possible for us to juggle more things than ever before. However, life lived at a faster and faster pace, with more and more balls in the air, comes at a cost. And the more we feel under pressure, the more we look for things that will make coping easier for us. It is clear that much of our economic behaviour is driven by our time poverty and our continual desire for things to be easier and more convenient.

Work

The central determinant of our time status is the role that work plays in our lives. Broadly defined, most adults spend the majority of their waking hours in work of some form or another. Whether it be paid or unpaid, recognised or unacknowledged, outside of the home or inside the home, most of us need to work. Nevertheless, many of our assumptions, attitudes and behaviours around work are deeply unhealthy.

Most obviously, the experience of overwork has become increasingly common. Over the last three decades, working patterns in Australia have undergone significant change, such that Australians now, on average, work among the longest hours in the developed world, with a greater tendency to work on weeknights and weekends and many employed on a casual basis only. Research shows clear links between these sorts of working patterns and unhappy family environments, characterised by some consistent elements: poor health for workers, strained family relationships, parenting marked by anger, inconsistency and ineffectiveness and, most worryingly, reduced child wellbeing.

Perhaps the greatest driving force behind increasing working hours in Australia is the incessant aspiration for a higher standard of living. Certainly, rising house prices have demanded Australians seek higher incomes; but at the same time, expectations about the size and quality of housing which many Australians want has risen dramatically as well. Similarly, Australian credit card debt, much of it spent on unnecessary consumption, is amongst the highest in the world. Although Australians have more stuff than ever before, they are also feeling more strain on their incomes.

For some, forced into casualised work, overwork has become an economic necessity; for others, driven by ideals of career success, overwork is a symptom of misplaced priorities. The label of 'workaholic' is sometimes seen as a badge of honour for 'hard workers'. However, like alcoholism, it can be a serious and widespread condition driven by deep emotional dysfunction that can be highly damaging to relationships and families.

By contrast, while many experience time poverty and overwork, there is also a significant portion of the population (much higher than is indicated by 'official unemployment rates') who have never worked, probably never will work and whose children will also probably never work. These are people with *too much time on their hands*, also a deeply unhealthy condition. Clearly, an economy that is characterised by both widespread overwork and entrenched generational unemployment is not a healthy one.

Of course, much of the work that is performed in our society is not even called work because it is not paid employment, such as the work of caring for children, the elderly, the sick and disabled and the work of clothing and feeding a family and keeping a household. To this day, most of this work is done by women. As money is really *the* measure of value in our culture, this unpaid work often goes unrecognised and unvalued. This means that many who are performing work that *really is necessary* often suffer from isolation, low self-esteem and economic hardship. This, too, can be another serious factor in relational strain, family breakdown and depression.

Leisure

The times we are not working (including home-based work), eating or sleeping can broadly be referred to as leisure time. How we choose to spend this time says a lot about our culture and is also an important factor in our economic behaviour.

The most glaring fact about contemporary leisure time in Australia is that most of it is mediated by a screen. The use of audio-visual media (TV, DVDs, internet, smart phones, computer games, iPads, iPods) occupies well over half the leisure time of the average Australian, with an average of over 1.5 hours of *leisure* time each day given just to internet usage. The Australian Bureau of Statistics found that while, on average, the amount of overall leisure time available to Australians *decreased* between 1997 and 2006, the amount of leisure time spent in front of a screen *increased* substantially. The areas of leisure time that suffered the most were sport and outside activity, talking, writing/reading correspondence, games, hobbies and arts and crafts.

This has a number of huge implications. Firstly, it means that our leisure time has largely become an act of consumption – we are consuming leisure products rather than actively pursuing our recreation. This is another major factor driving the technological consumption described above. Secondly, most of the screen-based entertainment we are consuming (including internet usage) either overtly or subtly reinforces and promotes the claims and demands of the consumer economy. If we spend hours each day receiving these sorts of messages, then we cannot help but be influenced by them. Thirdly, the amount of time given over to screens comes at a direct cost to the amount of time we actually spend in the presence of other people. At a time when our relationships need more work than ever, we are opting to turn to the alternative realities provided through a screen.

Technologically mediated leisure time also has obvious implications for our bodily health and there are clear linkages between our increasingly sedentary way of life and the rising incidence of obesity and diabetes. On the other extreme, many who have become concerned to maintain bodily health have become caught up in a cult of fitness that can also be time-dominating. Something as simple as providing healthy activity for our bodies has itself become an exercise in high consumption, requiring specialised clothing, specialist equipment, mediated by specialist trainers or instructors and pursued in specialist centres. It culminates in the daily spectacle of branded, lycra-clad people pounding on a running machine in a fitness club, listening to an iPod and staring blankly at a screen playing commercial TV. Much of the underlying drive of this culture stems not from a healthy concern for the body, but from an entirely unhealthy cult of the body beautiful, which is an extension of the culture of self. Such recreation does not 're-create' us; it deepens our alienation.

What Does the Bible Say?

It should be instructive to us that one of the first and most oft-repeated commands in the Old Testament law concerns how we use time; it is the command to *keep the Sabbath*. For many Christians today, the idea of Sabbath has tended to be trivialised and largely ignored. We have chiefly understood it as a command to be 'religious' for a day, which we subconsciously interpret as being boring and joyless. Because Jesus was critical of the legalism surrounding Sabbath-keeping in his own time, we have often interpreted this to mean that Jesus discarded the idea altogether. But he was not discarding the idea of Sabbath at all; he was, in fact, trying to reclaim its true meaning: '*The Sabbath was made for humankind*' (Mk 2:27).

The implications of the Old Testament command to keep the Sabbath are more far-reaching than we may have suspected:

i. The command to stop work for one day of every week is given to a people who have just been liberated from brutal slavery. As people who take two-day weekends for granted, we perhaps fail to see the radical social justice implications of the command that *everyone*, even slaves and foreigners, has a right to rest and *no one* should have to bear an endless burden of labour.

ii. The call to stop work is also a call to place limits on our production and our accumulation and, at the same time, to trust that there is enough abundance in God's creation to supply a day of rest.

iii. In Exodus 23 (10-11), the Sabbath principle is extended to creation itself, to let the land rest for one year in every seven, so that even the wild animals have enough to eat. This is an ancient recognition of the need to *place limits on human production* for the sake of ecological sustainability.

iv. The core commandment concerning the Sabbath is to keep it *holy*. Some strains of Judaism and Christianity have interpreted this to mean a day of seriousness and solemnity in which fun is absolutely banned. However, if we remember that the meaning of the word 'holy' is related to wholeness and healing, then we are really being commanded to take time to patch up the damage and scars we inevitably leave behind in our task-focused week. This suggests we should give recreation more serious thought: what things will help to *re-create* us – to make new our spirits, our relationships, our communities and our natural world?

v. Finally, the call to Sabbath is a call to step back from our blinkered, task-focused world of work and to 'remember': to remember the things that are actually important in life and to put things back into their proper perspective. Fundamentally, it is a call to remember our need of God.

The Bible has much to say about the place of work in our lives (for the moment, I am not making any distinction between formal and informal, or paid and unpaid work). Most strikingly, in Genesis 2:15 we are told that participating in work is fundamental to our created identity and purpose: 'The LORD God took the man and put him in the Garden of Eden to work it and take care of it' (NIV). Without some purposeful work to undertake, we are not fully ourselves. The Bible is eminently practical in recognising that we must work to sustain ourselves and our families and affirms that there is both dignity and meaning in labouring to live. Paul says that 'Anyone unwilling to work should not eat' (2 Thess 3:10). However, there is also recognition of the profound satisfaction that we derive from 'good work'; that is, work that is intelligently, skilfully and creatively undertaken in the pursuit of a good purpose (see for example, the celebration of intelligent and skilful work in Exodus 35 and Proverbs 31:10-31).

In the biblical vision, good work has a central place in the good life. However, as in all things, the Bible also lifts the veil on the dark side of work. For the fallen Adam and Eve cast out of Eden, the vision of good work had become a curse of futile toil. Their distance from God is immediately evidenced in their experience of work (Gen 3:17-19). In Exodus, the archetypal story of liberation for God's people is a story of liberation (amongst other things) from bad and exploitative work.

The Bible also asks critical questions about our *attitudes* to work, the sort of work we undertake and the *underlying motivations* for our work. Perhaps most importantly, the Bible is consistently scathing about devoting our working lives in the pursuit of a hollow dream of wealth, comfort and success: 'You fool!', Jesus says when he tells the story of a man who wasted his life on the pursuit of meaningless wealth and comfort (Luke 12:20). The biblical challenge is to think critically about how we invest our limited time and energy on this Earth:

> Why spend your money for that which is not bread,
> and your labour for that which does not satisfy? (Isa 55:2)

This prompts us to think about what things are actually worth our labour.

Moreover, not only is the Bible interested in the underlying motivations and purpose of our work, it is fundamentally concerned about the ethics of the work we do. There is no room in the Bible for any justification of work that involves harm to other people or to the community as a whole. Much of the work of the prophets is given to exposing and denouncing the systematic injustices of the 'respectable' world of commerce and business. In the eyes of the prophets, just because something is legal or even standard practice does not make it acceptable and does not change the fact that people are suffering because of it (see, for example, Isa 5:8-23, Jer 6:13-15, Ezek 34:17-24, Amos 5:10-12, Mic 2:1-5, 6:9-16).

Of course, the most profound ideas about work in the Bible are found in the New Testament. It is fair to say that New Testament writers show little interest in the minutiae of what work we do, or our place in society, even if we are slaves. Whoever we are and whatever our position, there is one big idea about work that applies to everyone: we are all called to participate in the work of God. This core idea is articulated in many different ways, again and again. Most profoundly, the resurrected Jesus says to the disciples in John 20: 'As the Father sent me, so I send you' (v.21). And what is Jesus' work that has now been entrusted to us? The Apostle Paul puts it most succinctly in 2 Corinthians:

in Christ God was *reconciling the world to himself*, not counting their trespasses against them, and entrusting the message of reconciliation to us. So we are ambassadors for Christ, since God is making his appeal *through us* (2 Cor 5:19-20)

The job with which we have been entrusted is nothing less than participating in the healing of the brokenness of the world. This means working to restore the broken relationship between humanity and God, the broken relationships between people, and the broken relationships between people and creation. This is such a big job that we all have a part – there can be no such thing as unemployment in the kingdom of God!

Paul expects that members of the Christian community will be involved in widely varying work. However, he urges all of them to think about how their work, whatever it is, can play some part in God's work. There are many jobs to be done and many different things needed; the most important thing is to think about our work in terms of *the contribution* it makes to the community (1 Cor 12:7). Paul talks of being involved in 'good works' (Eph 2:10), 'works of service' (Eph 4:12) and work that 'builds up' rather than pulls down (1 Cor 10:23-24). 'So then, whenever we have an opportunity, let us work for the good of all, and especially for those of the family of faith' (Gal 6:10).

How Might We Respond?

So, how do we use the biblical vision of work and rest to inform the choices we make in a world in which unhealthiness predominates in both? It is no exaggeration to say that the range of different actions we can take are limitless; from major life-changing decisions to small changes we could make today! Most of us would admit that we are unhappy about some aspects of how work and rest unfold in our lives. While this is an important and necessary realisation, the secret is to not try to 'solve' it all in one fell swoop. We need to think about what changes we can and should make carefully and prayerfully and learn to accept the things we cannot change (for the time being at least). Some things we will be able to act on immediately, but other changes will be ones we will need to work towards over a longer period of time, maybe even years. Below is a range of things to think through in the areas of work and leisure.

Work

1.Standards of living

If we are wanting our working lives to contribute to the greater work of God, then we cannot think about this apart from the issue of standards of living. How much do we need? How we answer this question is the central determinant of the major time allocations we will make in our lives between paid employment and other endeavours, and also in what type of paid work we pursue. Can we live with less? If we can answer yes to this question, then we can potentially liberate a whole realm of creative choices in the world of work.

2. Rethinking household work

When it comes to the work of the household, we have all got the wrong end of the stick. In the 20th century, men became the chief wage earners, divorced from the home, and household work became the lot of women, unrecognised, unvalued and isolated. With the rise of feminism, women, too, understandably wanted to abandon such stigmatised and isolated work, the result being a convenience economy in which no one wants to undertake the labour of running a home. Yet, while women have moved more into paid employment, they still bear an unfair burden of household labour.

However, there is perhaps no more satisfying work than the mutually shared and skilfully undertaken work of running a productive household economy that gives health to, and strengthens the bonds of, all its members. Indeed, it is hard to imagine – especially when one considers the raising of children and the care of the sick and elderly - more important work. Wendell Berry has connected the fragility of marriage in our culture with our disconnection from the home:

> The modern failure of marriage is a failure of our home economies. The practical bond of husband and wife in the home has almost

disappeared. It's a sacred and practical bond that gives order to a home, to family, to their descendants and to community. The work of the home is the health of love. And to last, love must enflesh itself in the material world – produce food, shelter, warmth, surround itself with careful acts and well-made things. Indeed, marriage is a union much more than practical, for it looks both to our survival as a species and to the survival of our definition as human beings – that is, creatures who make promises and keep them, who care devotedly and faithfully for one another, who care properly for the gifts of life in this world.

A healthy overall attitude to work requires *both men and women* to re-appraise much more positively the work of the household and to renew a sense of partnership in it. In most cases, this means men picking up their act at home! Indeed, many steps in other areas of this book (such as consumption and environment) require time, intelligence, energy and creativity be given to the household economy.

3. Non-paid work

If we are prepared to live with less, then one option that is opened up is the possibility of working part-time, to give more time to *good work* that is not paid. In Christian ministry circles, this idea has long been referred to as 'tent making', from the Apostle Paul's example of making tents to fund his work. However, tent making should not be restricted to 'Christian ministry'; it can be applied to volunteering in the community sector, working for a church community, building creative ventures in community, caring for family or pursuing a richer, more productive, more sustainable and healthier household economy (or combinations thereof). For some people, undertaking paid part-time work still needs to be 'meaningful' work for them; for others, as long as it pays the bills, is not unethical or degrading, then it is just fine.

4. Choosing paid employment

'What job should I choose?' This is the big question for many school leavers entering study or graduates entering the workforce. It is also increasingly a question for many who have been in the workforce for a long time. Everyone has different abilities, skills and education and the range of options in paid employment for each one of us is quite different. If we are seeking to align our paid work, as much as we can, with God's work, then there are a number of things to think through:

i. What are you good at and what do you enjoy? This is obviously an important consideration. Sometimes we really are called to undertake things we don't enjoy and don't feel particularly good at, but mostly God wants us to employ the gifts and passions we have.

ii. Is the work you are considering in any way damaging or harmful to people or creation? There are some jobs that Christians clearly should not do. Many people could agree that Christians shouldn't be involved in the arms industry, pornography, gambling or tobacco. Some people feel that Christians should have no part in advertising or speculating on financial markets. And there are large grey areas – what about the pharmaceutical industry, which has an appalling ethical record, but which provides a service that can (when done well) alleviate much suffering? These are thorny questions that cannot be answered here, but they absolutely should be the sorts of questions we are asking when making decisions about employment.

iii. What contribution does this work make to the world? Can we seek employment in activities that contribute something positive? It is no accident that Christians tend to be over-represented in the helping professions – doctors, nurses, carers, teachers, aid workers and social workers – and this is as it should be. However, we should remember that the world needs far more professions than these; we really do need good farmers, plumbers, mechanics, IT people, builders and thousands of other jobs that many people hardly consider important.

5. How do you perform your work?

Whether you choose to be a doctor, social worker, plumber or mechanic, the extent to which your work actually makes a positive contribution to the world depends entirely on *how* you do it. Most of us have experienced how, in a time of desperate need, a *good* doctor, mechanic or plumber – someone who does their work skilfully, sensitively, compassionately and with understanding – is something of a God-send. However, getting a *bad* doctor, mechanic or plumber at such a time can just add to the suffering. In essence, doing a good job, by a biblical definition, entails being fully conscious of the human dimension of our work – that is, its impact on people – and understanding that people are not just biological machines (for doctors), car owners, clients or customers. Often, performing work in a way that is more fully attuned to this reality will require doing things differently from the norm of how they are done in your profession and may even bring you into conflict with other workers or management who have different priorities. It should come as no surprise that trying to follow the way of Jesus in the workplace may well come at a cost.

Leisure

1. Making time for time

Many people reading this will scoff at the very idea of 'leisure' time because their time is under such constant pressure. But why? What is driving such busyness? There are periods and seasons for all of us when business necessarily claims a large portion of our time. But if this is a *constant* condition, we need to start to think critically about the damage it might be causing in our relationships, our spiritual life, our health and even on our ability to think clearly. Somehow, in some way, most of us have a need to reclaim some time and that will require re-evaluating the value of other things that claim it.

2. Re-think re-creation

How we spend our free time is a good indicator of what we really desire. The fact that such time is increasingly referred to as 'me time' is a good indicator of where our culture is at. We need to put some hard thought into asking what things actually re-create us; that is, what things make us new, as opposed to simply distracting or anaesthetising us. To what extent does our recreation contribute further to our alienation from others, and the ill health of either the body, mind or spirit? What sorts of recreation are good for our bodies, minds and spirits, good for our relationships, and good for the earth?

3. Re-creation that is not consumption

To what extent is our recreation dependent on acts of consumption? Are we dependent on someone else to supply us with a product or service to enjoy ourselves? Does having fun require spending money? We have been so shaped and moulded by advertising to desire the pleasures of the consumer economy that it is becoming harder and harder for us to conceive of activities beyond the entertainment industry as fun or interesting. But this is our great need: to actively reclaim control over that which is shaping our desires and to rediscover the enjoyment of so many things that come for free and which do not cost the earth.

4. Reduce screen time

We live in an age in which so much of our time is captured by screens. Whether we are watching TV or DVDs, surfing the internet, playing video games, engaging in text conversations or posting to Facebook from an iPhone, screens are beginning to dominate much of our relational time and mental world. While we might tell ourselves that some of this screen activity is 'social activity', it cannot help but have an impact on our immediate relationships. Moreover, the amount of time we spend with screens drives our massive over-consumption of the gadgets that hold them. It is also time that could be spent in any number of other activities, such as playing with the kids, gardening, sport and exercise, music and art, reading a book, doing some baking, visiting someone or just sitting still and having a good old-fashioned think.

5. Time disciplines

The idea of the Sabbath is predicated on the understanding that, left to ourselves, we do not necessarily do what is good for us (such as stopping work); we need some frameworks and disciplines that help us remember what is good, even if our immediate inclinations might not be to choose them. There are any number of ways in which the idea of Sabbath can be creatively applied to fulfil its original intention: that is, as a time for wholeness. Time disciplines can be framed either positively or negatively: nominating times of the week when you *will not* engage in a certain activity (such as shopping or looking at a screen), or times when you *will* do some things (such as family games, reading or prayer). While different personality types are inclined to different levels of structure in regard to time, nearly all of us benefit from having *some* time disciplines in place.

Of course, the elephant in the room is: what about time for God? If God is the voice that speaks out of 'sheer silence' (1 Kgs 19:12), how can he get a look-in amidst our worlds of perpetual noise and distraction? If there is one area where we desperately need counter-cultural time disciplines it is for prayer, reading the Bible and discussing our faith within our community. Our cultural programming tells us that such things are useless, but these practices are the only real oxygen there is to the life of faith.

Examples of steps people have taken

- Undertake an audit of the work of your home and discuss as a household. Who does what? What doesn't get done? How could the work of household economy be better shared and owned together?
- Undertake a time audit. Find out exactly how you are spending your time (you might be shocked) and use this as a tool for reflection about how you would like to spend your time.
- Nominate a screen-free (no TV, computer, iPhone, video games, etc.) time or times during your week (one night, two nights, a whole day, or more!)
- Institute some basic spiritual disciplines, setting aside a regular time to pray and read the Bible. Try to include some way in which this is shared with others.
- Commit to a retreat once a year.
- Cut back your paid work hours in some way.
- Institute an economic Sabbath day – one day a week when you do not engage in paid work or go to the shops – and commit to spending time with people and/or in creation, turning your attention to God (fun should most definitely be allowed!).

- Ask a friend or mentor to help you think critically about the work you do and the way you do it. What would it mean to follow Jesus' way in your workplace rather than conforming to the norm? What will be the cost of walking to the beat of another drum in your workplace?
- Take a year off your regular work to give time to something completely different.
- Re-think your paid work or career – why do you do what you do? Is this really where you want to give your precious time here on Earth? What is the cost to other things? Can you imagine your time being spent differently? What will it cost to make a change?

3. Consumption
A right relationship to things

What's the Problem?

It has often been noted that in modern democracies the role of the citizen is being reshaped into the role of the consumer. One of George W. Bush's first appeals to the American people after the September 11 attacks was to urge them to show their defiance by shopping. As the global financial crisis began to bite in Australia in 2008, Prime Minister Kevin Rudd urged Australians to do the right thing by their country and spend money.

At the deepest level, we have become a consumer society. No longer is the purpose of the economy to produce things for the good of the people; rather, the purpose of people is to consume things for the good of the economy. The mentality of consumption, indeed the *spirit* of consumption, lies at the very root of how we are being shaped and raised as people. To gain an appreciation of the extent to which our psyches have been moulded by consumerism, we need only take a look at the role of advertising in our culture.

Never before in history have people been subject to such a massive effort to mould the human mind. It has been estimated that the average urban Australian sees between 800-3000 pieces of advertising every day. Advertising is everywhere: on billboards, the sides of buses, the roofs of taxis, plastered over shop windows, in public toilets, on petrol bowsers. TV, radio and the internet are saturated with advertising, and we pay money to display advertising on our clothing. If you haven't noticed this extreme commercial bombardment, then that is an indicator of the extent to which it has been *normalised* for you. But whether you notice it or not, don't imagine that you are not influenced by it. In 2010, around $12.5 billion was spent on advertising in Australia. Why so much? Because it works.

The purpose of advertising is very simple: it is to manufacture discontent. The object of every advert is to make us feel a lack, to make us unhappy with who we are and what we have, and to offer a simple remedy through the purchase of a product. To do this, we are told thousands of stories about what life should be like and who we should be. Our attitudes to all of the most important things in life - self-image, relationships, sexuality, children, parenting, work, leisure, food, happiness, meaning, purpose, needs and wants - are being moulded to encourage consumption. The psychology behind modern advertising has become immensely sophisticated and subtle as hundreds of millions of dollars are poured into researching the most effective ways to pull the levers of the human mind and soul.

Perhaps most disturbingly, advertisers have discovered that children exert a very significant influence on their parents' purchasing behaviour – what is often referred to as 'pester power'. A significant proportion of advertising is now targeted at children; not just for children's products, but also for things such as cars, homes, computers and holidays. Marketers view children as a three-fold market: an actual market (for kids' stuff), an influence on the parents purchasing behaviour, and a future market. And so the consumer economy is applying itself strenuously to shape our children's minds. A report from the UK states:

> The result is that today's average British child is familiar with as many as 400 brand names by the age of ten. Researchers report that our children are more likely to recognise Ronald McDonald and the Nike swoosh than a representation of Jesus. One study found that 69 per cent of all three-year-olds could identify the McDonald's golden arches … [1]

Nowhere is the spirit of consumption more evident than in our consumption of technology. The explosion of consumption of computers, laptops, smart phones, iPods, iPads, plasma screen TVs, games consoles, palm pilots and more has ushered in a new age of constant consumption in which users feel their devices have become redundant within one to two years, irrespective of their working condition.

---

1 J. Freedland, 'Pester Power', *Resurgence*, March 2006. http://www.resurgence.org/magazine/article457-pester-power.html

Putting aside the social, psychological and spiritual effects of how these technologies have captured our consciousness, our technological consumption is having a very real impact upon the earth and upon the poor. These products are all combinations of plastic (derived from oil), minerals and silicon, all of which are mined from the earth, much of this in the developing world. Demand for technology products is driving a global mining boom. The effects of mining in the developing world have now been extensively documented. Whether in Latin America, Africa or Asia, mining has consistently had negative impacts upon local peoples and the environment, much of which goes unacknowledged, unmitigated and uncompensated. Moreover, the presence of large-scale resource extraction has been shown to negatively affect other sectors of the economy in many developing countries and to contribute to corruption and political oppression – what is known as the 'resource curse'. In the Congo, the mining of so-called 'conflict minerals', mostly destined for electronic devices, has added fuel to one of the most costly civil wars in human history.

Finally, as all of these products - bundles of plastic and heavy metals coated in toxic chemicals – are being made continually obsolescent through persistent upgrading, they must go somewhere. The problem of e-waste has reached colossal proportions: of the over 17 million electronic products thrown away *every year* in Australia, only a fraction is recycled in Australia. Most of it goes into landfill where heavy metals and toxic chemicals can leach into soils and groundwater. Some of it is diverted for recycling in China or West Africa, where components are burnt and disassembled by poor workers (sometimes children) in primitive conditions with no controls, with serious consequences for the health of workers and the health of soils and waterways.

We have been transformed into consuming machines, manipulated more than we know into continuous and ever-increasing acts of consumption, and the result is nothing less than catastrophic. We do not necessarily *feel* this to be the case, because the genius of the consumer economy has been, on the one hand, to rapidly *normalise* each new step up the consumer ladder so that we continually feel that our own consumption levels are merely treading water; and on the other hand, the consumer economy increasingly has *disconnected* and *abstracted* our consumption from the realities of their production. We generally don't think about the brutal minerals war in the Congo whenever we pick up an iPhone, but the two are linked.

Nevertheless, the evidence is incontrovertible. To feed our insatiable appetites, forests are disappearing, the earth is being dug up and mountains levelled; rivers are being polluted, diverted and dammed; soils are being exhausted; the oceans emptied of fish. According to the World Wildlife Fund's *Living Planet Report* for 2010, our consumption of the earth's resources began to exceed the planet's biocapacity – that is, the planet's ability to renew its resources each year - somewhere in the mid-1970s. Since then, world population has increased by around three billion people; at the same time, the *rate of consumption* – that is, the amount of the earth's resources each person uses – has also increased dramatically, nowhere more so than in the West. According to the Global Footprint Network, if everyone in the world lived like the average Australian does now, we would need between four to six planets to support us.

The damage of our consumer lifestyle is not just 'out there'. There is a growing body of evidence showing just how bad it is for us, the supposed beneficiaries. In 2006, the Australia Institute reported that though wealthier than ever before and consuming more of the earth's resources than ever before, 39 per cent of Australians felt their overall quality of life was getting worse. It is now commonplace for those working at the coalface of our social problems - psychologists, health specialists, family counsellors, drug and alcohol workers - to draw a link between the ill-health they are encountering and the predilections of a consumer culture. Indeed, it is hard to think of any modern malaise, whether physical, mental, spiritual, social or ecological, which is not in some way affected by the spirit of consumerism.

What Does the Bible Say?

The Bible is deeply concerned with our relations to material things. Indeed, the Bible sees the place of *material* things in our lives as a *spiritual* matter of the greatest importance. As we shall see, the biblical message offers a powerful critique of the spirit of consumerism; however, we should not make the mistake of leaping to the conclusion that everything it has to say about 'stuff' is negative. That is far from the truth. What the Bible says about our relationship to things is both more hopeful and more sobering than many would expect.

On the one hand, the creation stories of Genesis (chapters 1 & 2) insist that the material world is profoundly *good*, indeed, *very good*; and that human beings are creatures of the earth, made to enjoy the earth and its fruits. The idea that the human soul is somehow separate from its body is entirely foreign to the biblical worldview. While some religions and spiritualities (including some versions of Christianity) have seen the life of the body as something to be denounced and escaped, the Bible unashamedly affirms that the material pleasures humans can derive from good food, comfortable abodes and beautiful things are indeed pleasures that we are made to enjoy. The sentiment expressed by the psalmist is common to the Bible:

> You cause the grass to grow for the cattle, and plants for people to use, to bring forth food from the earth, and wine to gladden the human heart, oil to make the face shine, and bread to strengthen the human heart. (Ps 104:14-15)

Or the proverb which states:

> My child, eat honey, for it is good, and the drippings of the honeycomb are sweet to your taste. (Prov 24:13)

However, a proverb like this one is very quickly followed by another:

> If you have found honey, *eat only enough* for you, or else, having too much, you will vomit it. (Prov 25:16)

Here, in very short form, we have a summary of the biblical attitude to things: under the right conditions, the things of the world are good and to be enjoyed, *but* … and it is a very big 'but' … outside of the right conditions, our relations to things can do untold harm; indeed, it is one of the primal sources of human downfall. From beginning to end, the biblical story makes very clear that our access to God – our very salvation – is dependent upon establishing a *right relationship* to things. So what are the conditions of a right relationship to things?

The first condition is such a relationship can only be established in the context of *communities of enough*. The manna story of Exodus 16 sets the foundational ethic for the Israelites to observe if they are to be able to enjoy the Promised Land, the land of milk and honey. The ethic is very simple: none shall have too little, and none shall have too much. It is impossible to individually establish a right relationship to things in a context where others do not have enough. As 1 John bluntly puts it: 'How does God's love abide in anyone who has the world's goods and sees a brother or sister in need and yet refuses help?' (1 Jn 3:17).

The second condition, which flows from the first, is that we can never be in a right relationship with things when they have come at the expense of another. This is a major subject of the prophets' railings in the Old Testament:

> Alas for those who are at ease in Zion, and for those who feel secure on Mount Samaria […] Alas for those who lie on beds of ivory, and lounge on their couches, and eat lambs from the flock, and calves from the stall; who sing idle songs to the sound of the harp, and like David improvise on instruments of music; who drink wine from bowls, and anoint themselves with the finest oils, but are not grieved over the ruin of Joseph! Therefore they shall now be the first to go into exile, and the revelry of the loungers shall pass away. (Amos 6:1-7)

> As for you, my flock, thus says the Lord GOD: I shall judge between sheep and sheep, between rams and goats: Is it not enough for you to feed on the good pasture, but you must tread down with your feet the rest of your pasture? When you drink of clear water, must you foul the rest with your feet? And must my sheep eat what you have trodden with your feet, and drink what you have fouled with your feet? Therefore, thus says the Lord GOD to them: I myself will judge between the fat sheep and the lean sheep. (Ezek 34:17-20)

The biblical principle is crystal-clear: the 'rightness', or otherwise, of our acts of consumption can only be understood with reference to our neighbours. Consumption that comes at the cost of others is pleasure that comes with a bitter end. As the old proverb puts it: 'Better is a little with righteousness than large income with injustice.' (Prov 16:8)

The third condition, one that is particularly hard for our culture to grasp, is that there is such a thing as *too much*. As the proverb about honey graphically illustrates, things which may be good in and of themselves start to become detrimental to our health beyond a certain limit. Indeed, so dangerous is the state of too much that some of the strongest things the Bible has to say concern this state, and nowhere more so than in the words of Jesus:

> How hard it will be for those who have wealth to enter the kingdom of God! [...] It is easier for a camel to go through the eye of a needle than for someone who is rich to enter the kingdom of God. (Mk 10:23-25)

> But woe to you who are rich, for you have received your consolation. (Lk 6:24)

These are hard teachings and they have been more commonly sidestepped than dealt with; however, there is no way of avoiding the fact that Jesus, going against the grain of society, sees wealth and luxury as something perilous for the human soul. The consistent biblical insight is that deep in the human condition is a tendency to end up worshipping the things that we ourselves have made for our own enjoyment:

> Their land is filled with silver and gold, and there is no end to their treasures; their land is filled with horses, and there is no end to their chariots. Their land is filled with idols; they bow down to the work of their hands, to what their own fingers have made. (Isa 2:7-8)

This is put most succinctly by Jesus: 'For where your treasure is, there your heart will be also.' (Mt 6:21)

Finally, the Bible recognises what we can today see to be a glaring truth: that human consumption must be balanced against the needs of the earth itself. Although given to an ancient, rural people, there is already a clear recognition in the Old Testament law that while human appetites are unlimited, the capacity of the earth to supply them is finite. Therefore, a right relationship to material goods requires that limits be placed on the human production which supplies them. Thus, central to the Jubilee laws of Israel - the laws that defined Israel as distinctively God's people – is the command to rest the land every seventh year (Lev 25:1-7). The command makes clear that this is not just to ensure the future productivity of the land, but it is for the benefit of the whole ecological system, even the 'wild animals'. Human consumption is healthy when it is subordinated to the needs of the greater community of creatures (see the chapter on sustainability for more on this).

To sum up then, establishing a right relationship to things is an essential element of the goodness and the wholeness to which the Bible calls us. Our consumption affects, for good or ill, the most important things in life: our relationship with God, our relationships with others and our relationship with the earth.

How Might We Respond?

The very fact that we can now describe our culture by reference to its idolatry of consumption – a *consumer culture* – emphasises what a monumental task we have in trying to achieve a healthier relationship to things. The task requires both deep spiritual and mental struggle and critical awareness; it requires digging for information typically obscured from our view; it involves establishing new living habits; and it involves overcoming all manner of practical complexities. We should not expect to transform our material lives quickly. But neither should we allow the scale of the task to be an excuse for inaction. Somehow or other, the health of the world, and our own health, needs us to find new ways of being consumers.

The battle for your mind

Perhaps the most urgent task facing us is to become more fully conscious of the ways in which our relationship to things has been shaped by the culture and spirit of consumerism. This is a mental and spiritual exercise that has multiple dimensions. Firstly, it involves taking account of the ways in which we expose ourselves to advertising, through TV, flicking through magazines, the internet, or whatever. Jesus understood that achieving a healthy relationship to things is dependent on taking control of what we give our eyes to:

> The eye is the lamp of the body. So, if your eye is healthy, your whole body will be full of light; but if your eye is unhealthy, your whole body will be full of darkness. If then the light in you is darkness, how great is the darkness! (Mt 6:22-23)

This interesting little saying comes pointedly squeezed in between Jesus' teaching on treasure (where your treasure is, your heart is) and mammon (no one can serve two masters). We have very little hope of resisting the culture of consumerism if we continue to be immersed in its propaganda and worldview.

Practically, this needs to involve becoming more discerning, both in terms of quality and quantity, about what we are watching or looking at on screens (TV, movies, internet browsing, video games) or what we are reading. We need to ask, 'What is the effect of this on me?', and 'Is this a good use of my *time*?' (see previous chapter). Moreover, because it is impossible to escape the ocean of advertising and marketing, we need to get on to the front foot and become critical interrogators of the messages being continually blared at us: what is the story I am being told here? what motivations are being manipulated? (fear, desire?) what is the truth of the matter? Becoming more aware of the advertising around us ultimately means being more disturbed and angrier about the lies being sold us every day; it is a less comfortable place to be, but undoubtedly a healthier one.

Secondly, we need to become more deeply aware of the ways in which our desires for material goods, and our assumptions about what is normal, are shaped by the example of those around us. The genius of our culture of consumerism is that it is endlessly self-reinforcing. Each new increment of consumption, whether it is iPhones, Kindles or flat screen TVs, rapidly moves through the progression from luxury item, to normalisation, to *essential* ('I couldn't live without my iPad!').

We need to achieve a critical awareness of *just how much we have.* Two good ways of doing this are by comparing our lives to others today whose lives are literally a world away from ours; or comparing our lives to those of our grandparents when they were our age. If we pursue either of these exercises with anything more than superficiality, we will quickly discover that the material standard of living we consider normal is anything but normal; and, perhaps more simply but more profoundly, we will also discover that we do not *need* much of what we have. From here, we may be able to more critically reflect upon the big question of what effect our unprecedented levels of consumption has had upon ourselves. Are our lives really better?

Responsible consumption

We have been relegated to the position of consumers in what is a largely destructive economic system. This means that if we are seeking to move closer to the biblical vision of achieving a *right relationship to things*, we will need to practise our consumption with a level of care and conscientiousness that is entirely foreign to our culture. The catchcry of the Ethical Consumer Group is 'Your dollar is your vote.' How can we use our dollars to vote for a world in which people and the planet are respected and nurtured, rather than degraded and exploited?

The heart of responsible consumption is the preparedness to pay more for many of the things we buy. The reason our food, household items and technological appliances are so cheap is that we do not pay the true cost of production or transport: we do not pay the cost of extracting food, energy or resources from the earth in ways that are careful and sustainable; we do not pay a fair price for the human labour involved in production; and we do not pay the cost to the biosphere of transport-related pollution. However, there are options available allowing us to choose items that have been produced with greater care in one or all of these areas.

The simple principles involved in responsible consumption all derive from paying more attention to the things we buy. What stuff is this made from? Where does it come from? What was the impact of getting it? What role did people play in its production and how were they treated? How did it get here and what was the impact of its transport? These are basic questions but finding answers can be much more complex.

The easiest, and perhaps most important, place to start exploring these questions is in the area of food consumption. Choices for fair trade, organic, local, free range and minimally-packaged food products are all ways of expressing care for other people, other creatures and for the earth itself; however, they all cost more. There is now a wealth of resources available to help people begin exploring these sorts of choices, such as *The Guide to Ethical Supermarket Shopping*.[2] In effect, such a guide does the heavy lifting of sifting large amounts of complex information to help you make the best choices you can when confronted with the bewildering variety of products on a supermarket shelf. There are similar resources that have been developed for clothing and electronic goods.

Similar questions apply to household items and appliances; where did the materials come from and how where were they made? With these sorts of items, we also need to give attention to efficiency, life cycle and durability. How much energy or water does this product use? How long will it last? What will happen to it once its working life is over – can it be recycled? Once again, being prepared to pay more will allow us to make choices for more efficient, better made, better designed and longer lasting products.

Exploring the universe of responsible consumption is like following Alice down the rabbit hole. It is exciting and rewarding, but also often confusing. It requires thought and effort, not to mention lots of information. To be done well, keeping perspective is critical. It is simply not possible in this economy to transform ourselves into perfectly ethical and sustainable purchasers. The need for purity will only lead to paralysis, when what we need more than anything is movement.

Consume less

Given the nature of our economy, becoming more responsible in our consumption is an important way of taking care of our neighbour and the earth. However, on its own it is not enough. The end game of responsible consumption is to consume less. The world *needs* us to find ways to consume less. But this is easier said than done.

---

2 See www.ethical.org.au for more information.

The reality for most of us is that we tend to live according to our means. Indeed, with the advent of credit cards, we have been encouraged to live beyond our means. If our means expand, so does our consumption, and in the eyes of the world this is entirely how it should be.

The surest way to consume less is to begin to constrain your means. This is sheer madness as far as our culture is concerned and yet it rings true to the counter-intuitive gospel preached by Jesus. An easy way to begin to do this is simply by abandoning credit cards for debit cards (see chapter 7). Beginning to pay more for things for the sake of responsible consumption, as discussed above, will also have the effect of constraining your means. Opting to do less paid employment (see chapter 2) and choosing to be more deliberate and structured in financial giving (see chapter 5) are also decisions that have a similar effect. Being more disciplined in saving money (see chapter 6), especially if it is done by automatically redirecting a portion of your income out of your spending account, is also a helpful way of limiting your spending budget.

Re-use and repair

While responsible consumption often involves paying more, one of the best ways to reduce the impact of buying things actually involves paying less: that is, buying them second-hand. Every new purchase in the economy sends a signal through the market that effectively says, 'Make another one of those', which then sends a signal that says, 'Extract more of those resources'. When an item is bought second-hand, it short-circuits these market signals and does not stimulate new production; it also gives the materials used in the product a longer working life and keeps them from the waste pile that bit longer.

These days, there is a wealth of items that can be bought second-hand, in good quality and with relative ease: clothing, furniture, household items and appliances, computers, bikes and cars, the list goes on. Whether it is through op shops, second-hand stores or web-based markets, such as Gumtree, Trading Post and eBay, it has perhaps never been easier to find good quality second-hand items. Indeed, through groups such as Freecycle (email and internet), many useful things can be obtained for free.

Technology

Finally, it should be clear by now that we cannot talk meaningfully about responsible consumption today without talking about technology. Nowhere has our distinction between needs and wants become more distorted and nowhere has our desire for the latest thing become more frenzied. In this area, perhaps more than any other, we need to undertake some hard spiritual and mental reflection about what is driving our use and consumption of technology; do I really need this, how will it affect my life and behaviour?

Perhaps the simplest and most urgent task facing us is to stop upgrading and changing our devices so rapidly. Actually, the problem is not that we care too much about these devices, it is that we do not care anywhere near enough about them. Any electrical device – whether laptop, phone, monitor, or iPod – is a composite of the earth's finite resources and toxic chemicals, whose manufacture and transport requires significant output of energy that comes at a cost to the earth. If we accept (as most of us have) that we have become to some extent dependent on such costly goods, then we need to treat the work they do for us with far greater reverence and take their availability to us far less for granted.

It should be our aim to get a far longer working life out of electronic devices than the producers of these devices intend. Firstly, this means not continuing to be fooled into thinking we need something that we have never had before and learning to be content with what we do have. This means we will need to stop judging the adequacy of our devices by comparing them with what everyone else has.

Secondly, we could begin to do the unthinkable and look into having devices *repaired* when they stop working properly. This is becoming harder and harder and is simply not possible with some products, but still remains an option for many. It is a good example of the general principle that exhibiting care and responsibility *costs* – in time, money and inconvenience.

Ultimately, if we are applying a biblical lens, then we should be treating the purchasing of technology with a seriousness that is utterly foreign to our culture. If we do decide to purchase or replace a device, we might consider whether we really need the newest or latest thing. One of the by-products of such a rampant turnover in electronic goods is that there is a very large second-hand market of entirely sound equipment. As mentioned above, a second-hand purchase short-circuits the signal for more production and resource extraction and extends the working life of materials.

Examples of steps people have taken

- Purchase and begin using The *Guide to Ethical Supermarket Shopping*.
- Organise with a group of friends or church group to do the Ethical Consumer Group's 'Shopping with a Conscience' workshop (www.ethical.org.au)
- Commit to buying only fair trade tea, coffee, chocolate and cocoa.
- Set a goal of buying a certain percentage of meat, milk, fruit and vegetables from organic and/or local sources.
- Undertake a food miles audit of your pantry to build a picture of where your food is coming from. Begin to think of ways in which you could reduce those food miles.
- Undertake a packaging audit of your pantry – how could you reduce packaging through either alternate purchases or by buying in bulk?
- Try living by the 100 Mile Diet for one week. A web search will reveal lots of info on how to do this.
- Try the Zero Waste Challenge for one week. A web search will reveal lots of info on how to do this.
- Begin to grow some of your own fruit and vegetables.

- Learn how to manufacture at home one or two food items that you use regularly – e.g. bread, pasta, bottled tomatoes, jams and marmalades, cordials, wine and beer.
- Commit to trying to buy what you need second-hand before making a new purchase. Apply this to one, two or all of the following areas:
  - clothing
  - kitchen goods
  - household goods and furniture
  - vehicles
  - garden tools
  - electronic devices
- The next time you need to buy large whitegoods (fridge, freezer, washing machine), undertake research into which appliances are most energy and water efficient, will last longer, and which ones can be fully recycled. Be prepared to pay more for these features.

4. SUSTAINABILITY
An earth care-full way of life

What's the Problem?

In 2008, biologists Paul Ehrlich and Robert Pringle presented a paper to the National Academy of Sciences in the US in which they stated that, 'The fate of biological diversity for the next 10 million years will almost certainly be determined during the next 50–100 years by the activities of a single species.' Never before has it been clearer that the actions of humans are having a profoundly destructive impact upon the earth.

Perhaps the single most disturbing indicator of how bad things have become is the rate of species extinction. It is notoriously difficult to pin down just how fast species are disappearing from the planet due to the fact that we still only know a fraction of those that do exist. Nevertheless, there is a broad scientific consensus that current extinction rates are anywhere between 100 to 1000 times greater than rates characteristic of species in the fossil record. Put simply, over the last hundred years plant and animal species have disappeared from the planet on a scale comparable to the extinction of the dinosaurs, but at an incomparably quicker rate. And there is little doubt about the cause: us.

How are we doing it? That is no mystery; we have known for well over half a century how human action is resulting in rapid species extinction:

i. Over-exploitation of the earth's resources through the felling of forests, altering landscapes through mining, unsustainable fishing and hunting, extraction of fresh water for human use or consumption and the 'mining' of soil through intensive agriculture.

ii. Destruction of habitat, through the clearing of land and draining of wetlands for agriculture and urban development.

iii. Pollution of habitat through agricultural, urban and industrial run-off in the form of nutrient, effluent, toxic chemicals and heavy metals; the spread of non-biodegradable materials (especially plastics) throughout landscapes, waterways and oceans.

iv. Introduction of invasive plant and animal species, either by accident or design, into ecosystems.

v. Climate change, which has multiple, complex and often unpredictable effects on all sorts of plant and animal species and is now thought to have become the biggest driver of species extinction in the coming century.

Globally, the eco-region under most stress is that which is perhaps the least considered – the oceans. The 2005 Millennium Ecosystem Assessment noted that 'It is now *well established* that the capacity of the oceans to provide fish for food has declined substantially and in some regions is showing no sign of recovery'. Of the 232 fish populations for which there is data, well over half have experienced a collapse of 80 per cent of their population over the time humans have monitored them. Over-fishing and destructive fishing techniques have had the largest role to play in this decline. However, they are not the only cause; human pollution has also significantly altered the health of the oceans. In the middle of the Pacific Ocean there is a vast area called the Great Pacific Garbage Patch that holds an exceptionally high density of pollutants, most of it plastics that originated as land-based rubbish, brought by ocean currents from North America and Asia. There are similar zones in the Atlantic and Indian Oceans. In the Gulf of Mexico, there is a 'dead zone' of ocean more than 17,000 square kilometres that is virtually devoid of oxygen (hypoxic) due to the run-off of fertilisers from the Mississippi River. It is estimated there are over 400 such zones worldwide. However, these impacts are comparatively small when compared with the effect that increasing carbon in the atmosphere and rising temperatures will have on the health of the oceans.

Perhaps the next most stressed eco-regions are inland water systems: rivers, lakes, streams and wetlands. Not only are freshwater zones the areas of the world's highest biological diversity, they play a number of essential roles for all human societies. Most importantly, more than four out of every five humans depend on renewable inland water sources for drinking water. Currently, around 40 per cent of world food production comes from land irrigated from inland water systems, and freshwater zones are themselves a major source of food, especially for the world's poor.

It is estimated that perhaps as much as half of the world's inland water habitats were lost during the 20th century, primarily as a result of water extraction, drainage and in-filling, as well as erosion from vegetation clearing. Over half the world's major rivers have been severely damaged by the construction of more than 50,000 large dams (and possibly as many as 800,000 smaller ones). The Millennium Ecosystem Assessment considers that degradation of inland water systems is widespread, that the supply of freshwater is declining, and that water scarcity and poor water quality is an accelerating condition for one to two billion people.

Similar alarming stories can be told about the health of the world's forests, grasslands and drylands; however, there is not enough space here to cover all of these and perhaps there is no need – we get the picture.

What is becoming ever clearer is that not only have we made the earth less hospitable for so many of the other creatures who share it, but we are also seriously undermining the viability of our own species. It seems that in a 200-year fit of self-delusion, modern civilisation forgot what traditional societies have understood for aeons; that we depend upon, and are tightly bound into, the economy of the natural world. Modern farming has proceeded on the assumption that we can simply mine the soil of nutrients to maximise production, and then simply supply ongoing nutrient needs through synthetic fossil fuel-based fertilisers. The result is that each year about 10 million hectares of cropland are lost due to soil erosion worldwide. It is estimated that in the past 40 years as much as 30 per cent of the world's arable land has become unproductive. At the same time, the world's population – and therefore food production needs – continues to grow, currently set to reach around nine to ten billion by 2050, even as world oil production, upon which modern agriculture depends, begins to decline.

Reading through this litany of our environmental crisis is probably a harrowing experience, as is writing about it. If it is not a harrowing experience, then it probably means you have gone into emotional shutdown; a self-defence mechanism which kicks in as we try to avoid bad news. Indeed, this must be what has happened to us at a civilisational level. How else could we explain the continual failure of our society to face up to our global environmental predicament, when it has been known so well for so long? But we are not finished with the harrowing story yet. We cannot talk honestly today about our environmental predicament without confronting climate change.

None of the environmental challenges discussed above compare to the scale of the challenge posed by the current predicted scenarios of a warming planet, and all of them are significantly exacerbated by this change. Clive Hamilton writes:

> The shocking fact is that [the most] optimistic scenario would see concentrations of carbon dioxide in the atmosphere reach 650ppm [parts per million] (the pre-industrial level was 280ppm and it now stands at 392ppm). That level translates into warming of 4°C above the pre-industrial global average. As oceans warm more slowly, a global average of 4°C means warming of 5-6°C on land, and even higher closer to the poles. Warming on this scale and at the expected rate, would radically change the conditions of life on earth.

It is not possible to discuss here all the effects that a hotter planet and higher carbon dioxide levels would have on life on earth, suffice it to say they are legion. Beyond being hotter, with radically different weather patterns and rising sea levels, there are a host of other complex effects, such as acidification of the oceans and reduced capacity of plant life to photosynthesise. Hamilton writes:

> The impact of burning fossil fuels on the Earth's atmosphere has been so far-reaching that it is the principal factor, along with population growth, that has persuaded Earth system scientists to declare that the Earth has entered a new geological epoch known as the

Anthropocene, the Age of Humans. The Anthropocene is defined by the fact that the human imprint on the global environment has now become so large and active that it rivals some of the great forces of Nature in its impact on the functioning of the Earth system.

What Does the Bible Say?

It must be acknowledged that, for a very long time, the Christian church failed to recognise and teach the responsibility of humans to the rest of creation. Some strains of Christianity have even given licence to the wanton exploitation of nature. However, this is not due to any shortcomings about the Bible's teaching on the matter. Far from it. Contrary to popular belief, compared with other environmental philosophies, the biblical view of the natural world and the role of humans within it is the most positive, the most hopeful, the most challenging, and the view that most closely aligns to the actual reality in which we find ourselves.

The Bible opens with an amazing statement about the goodness of creation. Genesis 1 is not just an account of the beginning of the world: it is a hymn, a liturgy of praise to the creator God for the wonder of the world he has made. More than that, this Hebrew creation account is a direct challenge to more negative accounts of the nature of the world. In ancient Near East, the dominant creation story was the Babylonian myth, the *Enuma Elish*, which describes the creation of the world as a by-product of the bloody violence and gore of feuding gods. By contrast, Genesis 1 describes the world coming into being through a good God's *intention* – that is, as an act of love. According to Genesis 1, when we look at the natural world, we are seeing the product of God's love.

More controversially, Genesis 1 asserts that human beings have been given a special role within God's creation. Firstly, in verse 26, we have the astounding statement that man and woman are made in God's image; a profoundly radical statement of the dignity of every person, which is the origin (albeit mostly unacknowledged) of the modern conception of human rights. It then goes on to say that God gives humans 'dominion over the fish of the sea, and over the birds of the air, and over the cattle, and over all the wild animals of the earth, and over every creeping thing that creeps upon the earth.' Some people have claimed this gives humans a licence to plunder the earth, but nothing could be further from the truth. Even if we accept this English translation at face value, nearly all political authorities that have existed on the earth have felt the need to claim that their 'dominion' is for the good of all subjects, even if they haven't lived up to such claims. However, the Hebrew word being translated as 'dominion' or 'rule over' in many English Bibles – *rada* – is much more interesting and is better translated as 'mastery among', giving a sense of not only a special role for humans, but also their place amongst the other creatures of creation. Like a craftsman working with his tools and materials, God's intention is that humans achieve a level of skill, with an understanding and respect in working with creation that can be regarded as mastery.

Nevertheless, even with a less domineering reading of this text, within some forms of secular environmental philosophy the idea of a special role for the human species is still distasteful. On this point, however, the Bible is merely noting the actual circumstances in which we find ourselves. Only one species on this planet holds the future of the biosphere in its hands. The fact that earth systems scientists have named this 'the Age of the Anthropocene' strikingly confirms what was, to the biblical writers, already an observable fact. Humanity has frightening power in its hands, but it has not yet attained *mastery* of this capability; hence the litany of destruction related above. The biblical call articulated thousands of years ago has now become a categorical imperative: we simply must begin to attain mastery over our power or we will unmake ourselves and creation with us.

The account of Genesis 2 gives further depth to this understanding of the place and role of humans within creation. In this story, the first human – *adam* – is created from the soil of the earth – *adamma* – a word pun that profoundly locates man's belonging within the whole of creation, and that we will 'return to the ground (*adamma*), since from it you were taken' (Gen 3:19). The human is put into the Garden of Eden and instructed by God 'to work it and take care of it' (Gen 2:15, NIV).[1] We can immediately appreciate from this English translation that we are being instructed to care for the earth; however, in the Hebrew the vocation given humanity is all the more profound. The word for 'work' – *abad* – has the sense of meaning to *work for*, as a servant works for a master or king – that is, *to serve*. The word behind 'to keep' is the great Hebrew word, *shamar*. It is the same word used in the Aaronic blessing in Numbers 6:24, 'The Lord bless you and keep you', and contains the meaning of protecting, nurturing and raising to full potential. Yet it is the same word used to frequently instruct the Israelites 'to keep' or 'to observe' the commands of God or the dictates of justice. It is also used to mean 'to observe' in the sense of watching and understanding (e.g. Ps 107:42-43).[2] From this collection of meanings, we can see that to nurture and protect the earth also requires careful observation and understanding of its laws and especially its limits, that we might abide by those laws and limits. A fuller translation of Genesis 2:15 might therefore read, 'God took the human and set him in the garden to serve and to observe it'.

The recognition of humanity's dependence upon and responsibility to creation is a theme that continues throughout the Old Testament. In the books of the Law, which lay out a vision of the Promised Land, a land flowing with milk and honey, particular care is given to placing limits on human production. In the Sabbath Laws of Exodus 23 and Leviticus 25, the idea of Sabbath rest – a structured recognition of the need for healing and restoration – is extended from humans to the land itself, but also to animals, both domesticated and wild. The land is to be cultivated and worked for six years, but every seventh year is to be a Sabbath for the land: 'you shall let it rest and lie fallow, so that the poor of your people may eat; and what they leave the wild animals may

---

1 The NRSV translates this as 'to till it and to keep it'. The second part – 'to keep it' – is sound but 'to till it' is misleading, suggesting a narrow focus on agriculture that is not present in the Hebrew.
2 The phrase translated as "give heed" (v.43) in the NRSV is the Hebrew word *shamar* that appears in Gen 2:15. The KJV translates as 'observe'.

eat' (Ex 23:11). If the Promised Land is to remain a land of plenty, then human production and consumption must be subordinated to the needs of the broader community of creation.

More than that, the Israelites are warned again and again that the continued abundance of nature is dependent on following God's way. Should they fail to heed God's instruction on how to live in the Promised Land and go after false gods, the result will be that 'there will be no rain and the land will yield no fruit' (Deut 11:17). Once again, what the Bible asserted thousands of years ago we can now see as an empirical fact: the failure of humans to subordinate their production and consumption to the needs of creation – that is, *our greed* – has indeed contributed to drought, flooding, the disappearance of forests, the denuding of hillsides, the desertification of grasslands, the loss of topsoil, salinisation of soil, the collapse of fisheries and the list goes on. The words of the prophet Jeremiah have never rung so true: 'Your wrongdoing has upset nature's order, and your sins have kept from you her kindly bounty' (Jer 5:25, REB).

There is so much more in the Old Testament that testifies to the multilayered integration between our connection to God, to creation, and to our own wellbeing. The psalms, wisdom books and prophets are jam-packed with observations of nature that contribute to an understanding of God and understanding of the human predicament. Perhaps most startlingly, in the visions of Isaiah, the redemption of a fallen humanity happens alongside the redemption of a fallen creation. However, this a theme best explored in the New Testament.

Although it seems to have been, to a large extent, ignored by modern readers, the Apostle Paul repeatedly asserts that the redemptive work of Christ encompasses not just humanity, but all of creation: 'in Christ God was reconciling *the world* [*kosmos*] to himself' (2 Cor 5:19; see also Eph 1:10, Col 1:20). In Romans 8 he goes further, stating that it is obvious that creation is suffering ('We know that the whole creation has been groaning') and that creation's redemption is *dependent* upon ours: 'For the creation waits with eager longing for the revealing of the children of God

[…] that the creation itself will be set free from its bondage to decay and will obtain the freedom of the glory of the children of God' (Rom 8:19-21). Who are the children of God that Paul speaks of? Again and again, the children of God in the Bible are identified as those who are doing what God is doing: putting a broken world back together. In the language of Genesis, the children of God are the ones who reflect the image of God and attain mastery within creation serving and observing it.

Perhaps most significantly, the New Testament confirms emphatically what was already understood by the prophets – that the destiny of humanity is not to escape earth for some ethereal heaven, but that heaven is coming to earth. This understanding is the foundation of the way Jesus taught us to pray: 'Your kingdom come. Your will be done on earth, as it is in heaven' (Mt 6:10). It is also the final magnificent vision of the consummation of all things at the close of the book of Revelation:

> Then I saw a new heaven and a new earth; for the first heaven and the first earth had passed away, and the sea was no more. And I saw the holy city, the new Jerusalem, *coming down out of heaven* from God (Rev 21:1-2)

In summary, most of what the Bible asserts about the natural world is verifiable through our own observation and life experience:

1. Creation is deeply and profoundly *good* and it speaks to us of God.
2. Humanity has a special power in the natural world that no other created being has. Without *mastery* of this power, the impact of humans on nature is profoundly destructive.
3. The suffering of creation – a direct cause of human alienation from God – is, in turn, a prime source of human suffering.
4. The preservation and nurture of goodness in the natural world is dependent upon humanity attaining mastery of its power.

However, the Bible attests one more thing that is only knowable through its own revelation: God, through Christ, is himself working towards the redemption of all creation, and this is inextricably bound up in the redemption of humanity.

He has made known to us his hidden purpose ... to be put into effect when the time was ripe: namely, that the universe, all in heaven and on earth, might be brought into a unity in Christ. (Eph 1:9-10, REB)

If we are being redeemed by Christ, then we too are being called into his work of redeeming creation.

How Might We Respond?

The scale of the problem is enormous. The depth of our calling is profound. What are we to do? How do we as individuals and households begin the process of mastery of our own role within creation and take responsibility for our impact. It should not be surprising that we need to work on a number of fronts.

Consciousness and connection

Perhaps the greatest single obstacle to a perceptive understanding of the needs of creation and restorative action towards its health is the level of our disconnection from the natural world. We are the products of an urban, industrial, technological civilisation and every step down this path has been a step of progressively removing ourselves from the realities of the ecological community on which we depend. In our life, we do not *see* the complex and wonderful interaction of soil, plant, animal, fungus and bacteria, which is the basis of planetary life. We do not *see* the fine balance and fragility of it all and we do not see that our daily existence remains dependent on these wonderful interactions. How do we bridge this gap? We must get our hands dirty. Literally.

We cannot love and care for the natural world in abstract form (just as we cannot love and care for people in abstract form); we need to love, care for and be involved with *particular places*. Perhaps the best way to embark on this shift is to try, in some small way, to raise some of your own food from the soil. If nothing else, this will give you an appreciation of just how hard it is to grow food. Food production can be attempted in surprisingly small spaces, even balconies. For those without any space, there are an increasing number of community veggie gardens around. Urban zones also have a surprising number of natural spaces that require human care; parkland, remnant bushland, rivers and creeks, even waste lands. Many of these spaces have community groups, or 'friends' groups, who have taken it upon themselves to care for them and are always looking for new members.

Whether it is through a backyard garden or local bushland or some other means, we need to find ways to rebuild our consciousness of, and connection to, soil and growing things and the creatures that depend upon them. Once we begin to see on a local level just how big a problem weeds are, or how big a problem plastic is in the environment, or how hard it is to consistently raise good quality food, then we will begin to gain a much closer appreciation of the challenges being faced around the world.

Understanding our impact

As urbanites for whom food comes from a supermarket, electricity comes through wires, water from a tap, and waste goes into bins, we need to find ways of going back to the source and seeing more clearly just what all these things *cost*. Just as responsible consumption requires us to dig into the back-story of the things we consume, so we need to gain a clearer appreciation of the multiple ways in which we affect the earth. In particular, this demands that we begin to become more curious and more mindful about the materials we consume, about the treatment of animals, about the energy and water we use, and about the waste and pollutants we produce.

Every day we use and interact with, and dispose of, a host of materials that are all extracted somehow from the earth: food, paper, timber, plastics, metals, chemicals. Some of these resources are renewable and, if treated well, can be continually produced, while others are finite and can never be replaced. The impact of extracting these materials can vary enormously, from healthy and beneficial impacts to profoundly and wantonly destructive ones. If we know little about the materials and where they came from, and if they came to us cheaply, then the chances are that their impact has been more or less destructive.

It is not just the materials we use that have an impact. What do we know of where our electricity originates? Do we know how much water our households use and for what it is used? What do we know about our local water catchment and storage situation?

Clearly, we cannot become experts on the production processes of the whole consumer economy, yet if we choose to learn about one or two materials at a time (such as paper or plastic), if we share these with our friends and find out what they know and, most critically, if we just become *mindful* of what we are using, then it is surprising how much we can learn.

Reducing our impact

Perhaps more than anything else, as we have seen in chapter 3, reducing our impact on the planet requires simply reducing our consumption. The less material goods that come into our homes and out of them again, the less strain is placed on the earth to supply our wants. Also, as we have seen, there are many ways we can begin to exercise more care in our consumption of goods, whether food, household goods, appliances or consumer technology, that reduce the impact of that consumption.

Just as important as the hard stuff we consume is the soft and invisible stuff: energy and water. These days, we have become dependent on electricity in almost every aspect of our lives and it is electricity production, along with gas, which is the biggest single source (around one-quarter) of the greenhouse gas emissions that are driving climate change. Simply becoming conscious of our own household energy (electricity plus gas) consumption is a first step towards becoming more responsible, and the basic tool for this is the humble electricity and gas bill. As well as telling us how much we owe, energy bills also tell us exactly how much we have been consuming. Rather than seeing these bills as just another outlay, or even making sure we don't see them at all (if you are direct debiting), we can choose to use our regular energy bills as a critical tool in measuring the impact of our household energy consumption.

The second step is implementing measures to reduce energy consumption, and this requires working on two fronts: (i) behaviour change; and (ii) improving energy efficiency. Simply changing *how* we do things at home can make important differences to our overall energy consumption. This involves things such as turning off lights or heating/cooling in unused rooms, having ways of completely turning off all those devices on standby power (TVs, stereos, computers), having clear criteria about when heating or cooling is turned on, and making sure we have taken non-energy using measures first (putting on jumpers, opening/shutting windows and so on). These measures are all fairly simple but require the critical ingredient of *actually caring* about reducing energy consumption, which is where paying attention to bills comes in handy again.

Improving the energy efficiency of our households can be tackled on a number of fronts and can potentially lead to massive reductions in energy consumption. This can involve improving the efficiency of our homes themselves (draft sealing, insulation, shading, double glazing), choosing more energy-efficient appliances (especially paying attention to lighting, heating/cooling, whitegoods and TVs), and limiting the overall number of appliances in our households altogether.

The next major step in reducing the impact of energy consumption is to source energy from less damaging forms of supply. The most obvious, direct and perhaps satisfying way to do this is to install your own solar hot water systems and solar photovoltaic panels on your house. As well as completely cutting off demand for electricity from harmful sources such as coal-fired power plants, installing solar panels also makes long-term financial sense. However, this requires both owning your own home and having a certain amount of upfront capital to invest, which still precludes many people from such options. Another possibility is to choose 'green power' products from electricity and gas retailers. These products vary and require a bit of research, but in the case of electricity, generally involve notionally guaranteeing a certain percentage of supply from renewable sources, such as wind and solar. Once again, as in most measures of responsible consumption, this requires some time and research.

The final major area of energy consumption in our lives requiring attention is transport. Transport accounts for another major slice of global greenhouse gas emissions (about 13 per cent). We have been accustomed to shaping the geography of our lives based on the everyday use of the automobile and the availability of cheap petrol, and there has been very little incentive or need to keep things local. If you live in a major city, it is likely that work, social life, shopping and church all take place across a wide geographic spread. In what areas of our lives can we begin to reduce this spread? Where can we use lower impact public transport? Even better, in what parts of our lives can we make more use of our human energy by walking and cycling?

As with energy, the ready availability of cheap water in homes has accustomed us to profligate use of water. In 2013, the average Australian used over 270 litres of fresh water every day. Such vast amounts of water cannot be guaranteed for future generations on the Australian continent. Fears about water supply have led a number of states in Australia to build desalination plants, to provide drinking water from the sea, but requiring vast amounts of energy to do so and thus further contributing to climate change. As with energy consumption, reducing water consumption requires a mix of behavioural change (especially showers and baths), attending to the water efficiency of our homes (especially gardens) and appliances (especially washing machines) and, where we can, installing our own water supply infrastructure (water tanks and greywater systems). Once again, the humble water bill becomes a valuable tool for measuring our efforts at change.

Finally, we cannot think properly about reducing our impact on the planet without considering our waste. Everything about how we treat waste is designed to remove it safely out of our sight, and therefore our minds, as quickly as possible. The sheer volume of waste we produce is mind-boggling: over 18 million tonnes in Australia every year, the second-highest per capita waste production in the world (behind the

US). Most of this waste ends up in landfill, taking up valuable land, leaching toxins into soils and waterways, and emitting methane into the atmosphere. Once again, attending to waste requires working on a number of fronts:

1. Reducing the overall volume of waste by reducing overall consumption.
2. Changing consumption behaviour to reduce packaging waste.
3. Becoming better at recycling.
4. Reducing toxic waste (especially e-waste and batteries) and diverting it to specialist handling rather than landfill.
5. Where possible, keeping organic waste on-site or local through composting and ultimately contributing to healthier soils.

Working for healing

Ultimately, we need to move beyond the mindset of simply reducing the damage we do to the planet to becoming people who contribute positively to its health. The best place to start is at home or close to home. If you have a yard, you have a micro-ecology to manage. Rather than seeing yards as simply plastic spaces able to be endlessly moulded to our recreational fads, we can begin to see them as places in which to build healthy soils and raise food, places that trap and conserve water, and places which offer habitat to local bird species. In particular, there is much that can be done in closing the loop on so-called 'organic waste'. An aphorism of the permaculture movement is that 'there is no such thing as waste, only stuff in the wrong place' and this certainly holds true for organic matter such as food scraps, grass cuttings and tree prunings. Rather than sending organic matter to landfill where it produces methane, there is enormous benefit to be gained by keeping as much of it as we can on-site and putting it to productive use in composting and mulching. To be sure, this requires new perspectives, new skills and creative energy, as well as learning from many mistakes, but it is also tremendously rewarding.

Another place to begin working for healing is in local bushland and parklands. As mentioned above, many of these places have 'friends' groups or community groups, which either manage them or are seeking to improve their amenities, and such groups are nearly always crying out for new members and fresh energy. These can be wonderful places to learn about local ecology and local environmental issues from people who have been struggling at the coalface.

Moving further away from home, we can also seek to support the work of healing damaged nature through our money and political support. There are numerous non-government environmental groups who are playing a critical role in preserving and restoring threatened habitats and nurturing endangered species, and they are entirely dependent on public financial support. Including such groups in how we think about financial giving (see chapter 4) might be something we begin to consider. Likewise, there are numerous groups campaigning for public awareness or political change across a wide front of environmental issues; supporting these campaigns with our own time and energy (see chapter 1), as well as our money, might be something else we could consider.

Examples of steps people have taken
- Begin a household compost system.
- Switch to Green Power.
- Do an energy efficiency audit of your home. What measures can you take to reduce electricity consumption?
- Use your past water bills to set your household a realistic target to reduce water consumption.
- Next time you replace whitegoods in your house (washing machine, fridge, freezer), spend more money for greater water and energy efficiency. Top-range products also have more recyclable components.
- Do some research on the environmental impacts of everyday household consumption:

- plastic: production of plastic and where it ends up; find out about the Great Pacific Garbage Patch
- e-waste: find out what happens to e-waste and what the effects are
- pollution: find out about what things contaminate a local waterway and where they come from
- Find out how to responsibly dispose of e-waste (electronic goods, batteries, light bulbs) and institute household systems to regularise this.
- Find out about 5-10 plant species that are indigenous to your watershed. Try to grow one.
- Join a local 'Friends' group that is seeking to care for and restore local bushland.
- Go on a tour of an organic farm and learn about ecologically sensitive agriculture.
- Use a carbon calculator to determine your household's collective emissions. Where can you reduce your emissions? Explore off-setting those emissions you can't reduce.
- Reduce your meat and dairy consumption.
- Reduce your use of a car.

5. GIVING
Living with an open hand

In the last three chapters, much of the discussion about how we live in the areas of work and leisure, consumption, and in relation to the environment, has implications for how we make and spend money. It also concerns many other aspects of our behaviour and how we conduct our households. The next three chapters – discussing giving, savings and investment, and debt – focus directly on the question of money. Money is the mechanism of our economy and the greatest human force in the world today. We cannot begin to really think Christianly about home economy until we begin to think Christianly about money.

What's the Problem?

We live in a time when people are wealthier than ever before and yet still perceive that money is scarce in their lives. In 2002, a survey by the Australia Institute found that 62 per cent of Australians felt they did not have enough for 'what they really need'! Despite the fact that real incomes in Australia have trebled since the 1950s, the average Australian actually feels less financially satisfied than their grandparents felt. A study in 2004 found that while roughly a third of low-income families (35 per cent) understandably reported cash-flow problems, about the same number (33 per cent) of middle-income families did also.

Thus it should not surprise us that growing wealth has not been matched by growing generosity. While the total amount of charitable giving in Australia has been increasing due to population growth and economic growth, the proportion of the population who gives has actually fallen. Among those who do give, the average proportion of income given has remained steady at 0.9 per cent.

There is some reason to believe that Christians tend to be more generous than the rest of the population, but not by that much. There is little hard data for Australia, however, in the US, which is generally considered to have a more generous giving culture, Christians on average give around 2.5 per cent of their income (it was about 3.3 per cent during the Great Depression).

From one perspective, this is a remarkable phenomenon. Never before in history have people had such a secure provision of their material needs; indeed, our experience of material prosperity is more accurately one of superabundance, leading to excess. One might think that under such conditions those who are called to 'love their neighbour' as the central tenet of their faith would be liberated to a generosity such as the world has never known. Instead, perceptions of financial scarcity are as strong as ever, perhaps even stronger.

Of course, what has happened is quite easily explained. Increasing material prosperity has not been accompanied by a sense of material satisfaction, but merely a continual ratcheting-up of perceptions about the standard of living necessary for human happiness. This is a well-known phenomenon to economists who have long understood the processes of *habituation* (the process by which we continually make any rise in wealth the new normal) and *rivalry* (the process by which we define our own position by comparison with others). That is why first year economics students learn that the purpose of their science is not to ensure the provision of limited needs, but the provision of *unlimited wants*.

All this serves to make a very simple point: we cannot talk meaningfully about giving without also discussing perceptions of standards of living. How much do we need and how much can we share with others?

Imagine two families living on the same income and at basically the same material standard of living. One of these families is acutely aware of the prosperity of the Joneses next door, the new SUVs of school mums and the overseas trips and real estate acquisitions of workmates. They are feeling the pressure of modern life, always wondering how they will pay for the things they feel they would like to (or should) be doing. The second family has spent some time living in a developing country and is acutely aware of just how enormously wealthy and comfortable their lives are. You do not need to be a rocket scientist to figure out which of these two families is likely to be more generous in giving. Perception is everything.

However, there are some other external factors that also affect how we think about giving. One has been the rapid proliferation of charities representing a bewildering array of causes: between 2000 and 2013, over 10,000 new charities were started in Australia. This means that there is a rising number of charities dependent on attracting donations from a limited pool of generosity. In this increasingly competitive environment, there has been strong movement for charities to adopt aggressive marketing strategies, frequently outsourcing their fundraising to specialist commercial firms. We are all familiar with those annoying phone calls while trying to cook dinner and semi-personalised mail filling our letterboxes and email inboxes. The result is that, at the precise time when people are feeling increasingly uncertain about their ability to be generous, they are also feeling overwhelmed by the number and array of charities using guilt and pressure tactics to try to elicit a donation. For many, this predictably leads to paralysis. When you don't know what to do, it is easiest to do nothing.

Our giving, or lack of giving, is also affected by the geography of our lives. Suburban existence is quite effective at segregating social classes so that our lives tend to be grouped with people of roughly similar socio-economic positions. Unless you are particularly perceptive or looking for it, most people see very little of others for whom day-to-day life is a struggle. How much less do we comprehend the lives of those in the urban slums of Kenya, Haiti or Bangladesh? Indeed, if you spend most of your down time watching junk TV or shopping on the internet (see chapter 1), then you could be tempted to think that an affluent middle-class existence is 'normal'. Clearly, our awareness and perception of need has a massive influence on how much we give and what things we support.

Finally, it is important to acknowledge some of the generational differences in giving. It has been widely recognised that Gen Y and, to a lesser extent, Gen X, tend to give in very different ways to previous generations; they are much more likely to buy products where proceeds go to charity (t-shirts, wristbands etc.), more likely to give to internet-based crowd-funding appeals, and generally preference giving where they can personally see a direct impact. However, the overall generosity of Gen X and Gen Y is significantly less than previous generations. A 2012 study in the UK found that the generation of people over 60 – those known as the builders and boomers – were six times more generous than those under 30 – Gen Y. It reported that, in 1980, 23 per cent of under 30s gave to charity but in 2010 that figure had fallen to just 16 per cent. Similar observations have been made across the English-speaking world.

If this trend continues, then it seems clear that the charitable sector faces a long-term income crisis as the older and more generous generations pass away. This is already the case in many churches, where it has long been evident that Gen X and Gen Y (those who remain in the church) have been far less diligent and serious in their financial commitment to their own faith communities.

What Does the Bible Say?

Before we can properly understand what the Bible teaches about giving (or investment and debt), we have to understand what it teaches about money. The difficulty is that the Bible says so much about money that it is almost impossible to do it justice here. For our purposes, it is perhaps most important to gain a clear view of the teaching of Jesus on money, as it is strong and consistent. Indeed, Jesus teaches about money more than any other subject other than the kingdom of God. Clearly, he sees this as a subject that we must come to grips with if we are to follow his Way.

Halfway through the Sermon on the Mount, Jesus drops a bombshell: 'You cannot serve both God and Money' (Mt 6:24, NIV). The language is uncompromising. He doesn't say it is hard to do, or unwise to attempt; it simply cannot be done. At this point, we really should be sitting up and taking notice. What does he mean?

What is particularly striking about this saying is that Jesus chooses a very particular way of naming money: *mammon*. Mammon was an Aramaic word for referring to money or riches that held strongly negative connotations – it is thought to derive from the Aramaic term (*mumu*) which means 'that in which one trusts'. But Jesus' choice of the term goes beyond normal usage; in this teaching, mammon is personified, given the full force of idolatry and put in direct opposition to God: 'You cannot serve both God and mammon'.

When Jesus identifies money with mammon, he is powerfully drawing our attention to a fact that we should all be able to realise, simply by looking at the world or paying attention to our own lives, that money has become much more than just a means of exchange. It has become a *spiritual force*. That is, Jesus is locating money in the same category of things discussed by the Apostle Paul when he states: 'our struggle is not against enemies of blood and flesh, but against the rulers, against the authorities, against the cosmic powers of this present darkness, against the spiritual forces of evil in the heavenly places.' (Eph 6:12).

In recognising that money is a spiritual force, we are acknowledging not only that money is a crude form of power that humans can wield to gain 'possession' over things, even over other humans, but that it is also a form of power liable to possess the possessor and none of us is immune. More than that, Jesus understands that we place a very deep trust in money. Although we talk of faith in God and we have hopes in the support of family and friends, our actions tend to belie the fact that the one thing we really trust to help us or secure our future is money.

That is why Jesus unmasks money as mammon – a false god that promises life and leads us to death. Money has its own logic and its own commandments, and we simply cannot serve that logic and serve God at the same time. The two are irreconcilable.

This is the starting point that lies at the heart of understanding all of Jesus' teachings on money. We all need money. It is impossible for us to live without it. But if we are not to be led astray by it, and even more so if we are to put it to some good uses in the world, then we must first learn to see it aright. After that, we need a set of practices that will help break its spiritual power, which brings us back to the Bible's teaching on giving.

A biblical view of giving must begin with the Hebrew ideas of tithing and first-fruits offerings. Unfortunately, these ideas have been caught up in a surprisingly bitter and turgid debate within some parts of the church (especially in the US) about whether the tithe is a biblical 'law' that still applies to Christians or whether we are 'liberated under the new covenant'. Both these positions miss the point. The Hebrew 'law' represents a vision of life whose underlying *principles* remain consistent through the Old and New Testaments, even if the details are no longer relevant. I believe this is true of the tithe and first-fruits offerings.

The essential idea behind the tithe (which simply means 'a tenth') is the simple acknowledgement that all we have comes from God. Leviticus 27:30 states: 'All tithes from the land, whether the seed from the ground or the fruit from the tree, are the LORD's; they are holy to the LORD.' By giving a tenth of their incomes 'back to God', the ancient Hebrews were simultaneously bearing witness to this fact, demonstrating their gratitude for what they had, and (as with the Sabbath laws) declaring their trust in a different system that was not defined by 'every man for himself'. This statement of both trust in and commitment to God's economy is taken further in the first-fruits offering (Deut 26:1-11). The simple idea here is that what was given to God deserved to come from the first of what they got and not from what was left over (if anything) once they had used what they wanted.

While the ancient Hebrews saw the tithe as giving 'back to God', the way this was practically fulfilled was to give to 'the Levites, the aliens, the orphans and the widows' (Deut 26:12). Put simply, giving was to be put towards God's healing work in the world. This short list in Deuteronomy has two sub-categories of healing to be supported: (i) 'the Levites', or those who are tasked with leading, supporting, enriching and guiding the community of faith; and (ii) 'the aliens, the orphans and the widows', which is to say, the disadvantaged, vulnerable, exploited and poor.

Essentially, the tithe represents a structured financial commitment to make God's work in the world an ongoing part of our household economy. It is also a direct decision *against* the power of mammon, which urges us to hold on to our money or spend it on ourselves.

Interestingly, however, when we reach the New Testament, Jesus actually shows very little interest in tithing. This is probably because of some specific historical factors (such as the exploitative economics of the Temple system and the legalism of Pharisaic Judaism), but it also reveals some of the operation of the spiritual economy that lies behind the monetary economy. When Jesus is critical of the Pharisees in Matthew 23, he endorses their tithing but rejects their failure to grasp the heart of the matter: 'For you tithe mint, dill, and cummin, and have neglected the weightier matters of the law: justice and mercy and faith. It is these you ought to have practiced *without neglecting the others*.' (v.23).

In a context where tithing had become an exploitative form of public piety, Jesus shows more interest in the idea of 'almsgiving'. The English word 'alms' stems from the Greek '*eleos*', which means mercy. Almsgiving is simply the response of mercy when confronted with need and Matthew's gospel sets a demanding standard: 'Give to *everyone* who asks from you, and *do not refuse anyone* who wants to borrow from you' (Mt 5:42). Once again, the lack of qualification in this text is something we find troubling, but what is clear is that Jesus is calling us to more than a 'crumbs from the table' response to need; he is calling for *radical and spontaneous generosity.*

It is not hard to see that such a response is basically a call to a fuller identification with the humanity of others; a fuller compassion and empathy towards the pain and need of others. What is interesting is that Jesus is not just interested in what we give, but *how* we give:

> Beware of practising your piety before others in order to be seen by them; for then you have no reward from your Father in heaven. So whenever you give alms, do not sound a trumpet before you, as the hypocrites do in the synagogues and in the streets, so that they may be praised by others. Truly I tell you, they have received their reward. But

when you give alms, do not let your left hand know what your right hand is doing, so that your alms may be done in secret (Mt 6:1-4).

It seems that Jesus is not just interested in the *exterior fact* of our generosity, but also the *interior posture* of it. He is well aware that we may give for reasons other than simple generosity - whether for social recognition, self-justification or even as a form of power over the recipient – and so he demands a practice of giving that leaves ulterior motives unfulfilled.

In these two short but central passages of the Sermon on the Mount, Jesus sees giving as an act that has significance not just for the recipient, but also for the giver. In asking us to be ever-ready to simply give money away, Jesus is asking us to contravene the laws of mammon. If we can do that, then we have broken the spiritual power of mammon and rendered it mere money again. At the same time, when we give money away our use of money becomes another dimension of the core spiritual movement of the gospel: that of dying to oneself.

If any want to become my followers, let them deny themselves and take up their cross and follow me. For those who want to save their life will lose it, and those who lose their life for my sake will find it. For what will it profit them if they gain the whole world but forfeit their life? (Mt 16:24-26)

It is not just an act of self-negation, it is an act of *self-giving*, a movement towards another. Our use of money becomes an act of love and a manifestation of our salvation. Once again, we can see how the spiritual and material are inextricably intertwined in the gospel.

The Apostle Paul also points to Christ's self-giving – 'though he was rich, yet for your sake he became poor' (2 Cor 8:9) – as the example that should lie at the heart of our financial giving. Interestingly, however, the attitude of generosity he is exhorting the Corinthians to cultivate is more an act of equity than of charity:

I do not mean that there should be relief for others and pressure on you, but it is a question of a fair balance between your present abundance and their need, so that their abundance may be for your need, in order that there may be *a fair balance*. As it is written, 'The one who had much did not have too much, and the one who had little did not have too little.' (2 Cor 8:13-15)

It is instructive that in this teaching Paul is directing his readers back to the principles of the manna in the wilderness, where there is a free-flowing economy of enough, but stored wealth turns rotten.

How Might We Respond?

The six-million-dollar question for most people who want to take the biblical challenge of giving seriously is, 'How much should I give?' But before tackling this thorny question, it is perhaps helpful to first think about *how* we give. In particular, it is worth thinking through the roles that structured giving and spontaneous generosity play in our lives, as these inform the question of how much we give and also concern the deeper spiritual role that giving plays for us.

Structured giving vs spontaneous generosity

The old Christian practice of tithing – that is, of structured, regular giving – is one that is becoming less adhered to by upcoming generations, yet it is a practice that has immense spiritual and practical value. Spiritually, tithing requires a clear and ongoing decision to give up 'ownership' of a portion of your income; or more correctly, to acknowledge who is the true owner of our wealth. It is not something done on a whim, or intermittently, but represents a *decision* and a *commitment* to serve God with your finances, irrespective of feelings or circumstances. Seen in its full light, the tithe is the first line of a household budget, something that comes out before rent and food and even before tax. It may seem a small point, but it is spiritually significant that we render unto God before we render under Caesar; hence the long-standing practice of Christians tithing on *gross income* rather than net income. One of the advantages of electronic transfers and automatic recurring direct debits is that it is now very easy to turn such spiritual commitments into practical reality. We can effectively structure our accounts so that the money never was ours.

In this respect, the tithe is really a voluntary decision to forego a portion of your income. And it means, if practised in this way, that it necessarily represents a reduction in disposable income. This means less money to spend on things, requiring a bit more discipline and frugality in consumption patterns.. It means voluntarily placing a limit on our material standard of living.

Let us be clear: in our consumer culture such a decision goes deeply against the grain and is becoming psychologically harder and harder to make, even though we have a standard of living that permits it more than at any time in history. And yet we have a desperate need to restrain our consumption, for the sake of our own spiritual and physical health and for the sake of the planet (see chapter 2). Tithing is not a dour act of old-fashioned religion; it is a profound act of spiritual health. And we have not yet even mentioned that regular dependable giving, compared with sporadic and fluctuating giving, is by far the most helpful way to support good work in the world. From the perspective of churches, charities or development organisations that depend on giving, structured giving is by far the most preferable.

Seen in a fresh and new light, shorn of some of the dour legalism of the past, tithing is certainly a practice that should be given serious consideration by all Christian households. But we should not make the mistake of thinking that it fulfils the entire spiritual economy of giving found in the Bible. Indeed, there are some spiritual dangers associated with tithing: it can become an act of self-righteous religiosity by which we take pride in our spiritual superiority to others, especially if it is performed publicly, and it can become a tool for hardening our hearts to people in need; 'I have given my tithe already, so I do not need to extend my hand to you'.

It is for these reasons that Jesus urged his followers to go beyond tithing and to also give *alms*. Whereas the tithe is an important act of decision and commitment to give to God, almsgiving is a spontaneous act of generosity impelled by compassion and mercy. It is uncalculated and therefore more risky. Whereas tithing involves a deliberate decision about how we give our money, opportunities for spontaneous generosity are often thrust upon us.

Perhaps you will have noticed, as you read these accounts of structured giving and spontaneous generosity, that you are naturally inclined towards one more than the other. Some people find structured giving easy and spontaneous generosity immensely hard. Others struggle to get ordered or disciplined enough to give regularly but give freely when confronted with need. The biblical witness attests that *we need both*. They roughly equate to serving God with both head and heart. On its own, spontaneous generosity is undependable and easily turns into laxity. Structured giving on its own can tend to harden the response of compassion and mercy. This means most of us will need to actually *cultivate* a practice of giving that does not come naturally.

To whom do we give?

Traditionally, the Christian tithe has been solely a financial commitment to the local church. However, remembering the purpose of the tithe in the Old Testament - to support 'the Levite, the alien, the orphan and the widow'; in other words, supporting God's healing work in the world - there is no reason to think of tithing exclusively in relation to the local church. There is increasingly some reluctance among some Christians to tithe solely to the church, and for some understandable reasons. In Western countries such as Australia, the church has generally become an economically bloated institution. There are too many churches with massive resources tied up in expensive building projects and top-of-the-shelf audio-visual systems, which in turn demand a monopolistic claim to their members' giving. While these would all claim that the buildings and sound systems are to further God's work, it is hard not to be dubious about the extent to which these end up being well-resourced, self-funded services for middle-class Christians. Similarly, the major denominations have developed high-cost bureaucracies of professionalised staff which demand an increasing drain on congregational giving.

Moreover, there are a plethora of organisations out there we should think of as, in some way, participating in God's healing work in the world: aid and development organisations, humanitarian and relief organisations, welfare and charitable services. And there is no reason why we should restrict this definition to just Christian agencies. Wherever there is genuine work of healing and restoration going on, people are participating in God's work, whether they know it or not.

This is a tricky issue for which there is no clear answer. Clearly, we cannot expect or hope for dynamic churches unless their members are prepared to support them financially. If we yearn for churches to express a more authentic form of community, then this necessarily includes and requires some level of financial community. Certainly, younger generations of Christians will need to move beyond the seemingly entitled expectation that church will be there to meet their needs.

On the other hand, the reality is that many might find themselves in churches to which they have a basic commitment, but on whose financial decisions they may not fully agree. This is simply a matter for *ongoing discernment*: how do you balance the need you see within your faith community with the need you see in the world? It is likely your discernment of such need will fluctuate and change over time and there is nothing wrong with that.

The question of where we direct our giving is particularly challenging these days with respect to spontaneous generosity. With so many aggressive charities calling us at dinner-time to ask for money, it seems clear that Jesus' injunction to 'give to everyone who asks' cannot be followed literally. If we did so, we would end up directing most of our giving to causes and organisations – some genuine and some more questionable – that ultimately serve and benefit our already affluent communities. This is especially the case for the amount of money we are increasingly being asked to direct into expensive medical research for conditions that afflict a very small percentage of humanity (and only those who are located in wealthy countries) while millions of children continue to die from simple lack of access to clean water, low-cost vaccines and oral rehydration formulas. Most of the suffering in the world is caused by things for which the solutions require no research and are often inexpensive.

The very aggressiveness of the charity market means we are forced to have to apply some filters to our generosity. A simple filter I have found useful is that I refuse to give to any charity that uses methods I disapprove of – invasive, aggressive or manipulative marketing – and I tend not to give to First World causes unless there is a personal connection to either the cause or the person raising the money. That cuts out a lot, but it still leaves a huge number to choose from.

So far, I have only talked about charities, however, spontaneous generosity is perhaps best directed to local and personal situations that you come across in your church, school community or sports club. It has been my experience that unlooked-for financial help in a time of need – even if it is unable to fully meet the need – can be a powerful vehicle of grace that not only provides practical help, but also reminds someone of the transforming truth that they are not alone. *How* such giving is done can be very important, but it is very difficult to come up with any rules. Sometimes, especially in situations where receiving a financial gift would be awkward for someone, an anonymous gift – an envelope in the letterbox – can be the best expression of grace. Anonymity can also be an important spiritual discipline for ensuring that our giving isn't serving the two-fold purpose of increasing our kudos or leverage with that person. At other times, especially in church communities, it is appropriate that a gift is given as recognition of the fellowship and community shared with that person. Once again, there are no rules; all we can say is that *discernment* is required.

What about beggars? This can be a pressing question for those who live or work in the centre of a city. Here we are confronted by the direct appeal of people who are poor, a combination of need and human interaction against which we are otherwise largely insulated. Surely this is the moment that most closely fits Jesus' call for *eleos*? However, one factor complicating the dynamic of begging in our times is the suspicion that its purpose is to feed a substance addiction. I have worked for a number of years in a street mission and know that such a suspicion is often true. Yet, how do we weigh such a consideration in deciding whether or not to give? On the one hand, we can say that giving our money to temporarily feed an insatiable addiction is a complete waste and not benefiting anyone. That is probably true enough. On the other hand, need is need and is it our place to judge? Furthermore, one of the challenges presented by begging is that, usually, we do not *know* anything about the person or their situation, whatever our suspicions and assumptions. Surely, Jesus' commands to show mercy and withhold judgement both come to a point on this issue?

Some people in this situation have decided they will not give money to feed an addiction, but instead offer to buy the person a meal or a coffee. Such an act combines a material gift with the gift of time and attention and can be a wonderfully human interaction in an otherwise heartless city. However, it is not always possible to do this and sometimes such an offer is frankly resented by a beggar who just wants the money. To sum up then, it is very difficult to come up with any clear guides for action that will serve in all cases. The ancient act of begging remains a confronting and disturbing challenge to our consciences and the words of Jesus only serve to sharpen the challenge. Perhaps the only really clear principle is that we should never *ignore* a person who is begging; whatever our decision, we should always remain *disturbed* by the human plight it represents.

How much?

Finally, the big question: how much should we give? Perhaps the answer should simply be, 'As much as we can'. Experience tells me, however, that this is much too vague for many people. In my experience, the figure of ten per cent – a tithe – provides a very good baseline for thinking about giving. There is no reason to think of ten per cent legalistically as some magic number God requires of us; however, it serves the very practically useful function of providing a *goal* for *structured giving* that is both challenging and achievable. From such a base, further giving in the form of spontaneous generosity begins to really deserve the name 'generosity'.

In his book, *Rich Christians in an Age of Hunger*, Ronald Sider advocated the idea of a graduated tithe. In this model of giving, Sider sees ten per cent as a *baseline aspiration* for all Christians, but he saw no reason to stop there. If your income increases and you are already living comfortably, why only maintain giving as a proportion of a rising standard of living? Why not be content with what you have and increase the proportion? For example, if your income increases by $10,000, perhaps think about giving away 15 per cent of your income. If it goes up by another $10,000, then perhaps consider making it 20 per cent. The particular numbers or percentages are not important – what is important is that Sider has located giving as connected to the question of standard of living. Is there a point where we can say, 'We have enough, we need no more. Anything more we receive can go to others at no cost to ourselves'? If we cannot answer yes to this question, then we are in spiritually dire straits.

Examples of steps people have taken

- Commit to give away a specific percentage of your annual income and develop a plan of how you will give and to whom.
- Explore the idea of a graduated tithe: determine a base income at which you will give away a base percentage of your income (e.g. ten per cent). If your income rises (faster than inflation), then increase the percentage you give.
- Decide to make one generous gift in the year, beyond any giving plan, to an organisation or person you feel is doing good work in the world yet is little recognised and in need of encouragement.
- Consider adding one new dimension to your giving this year (whether by redistributing what you already give or increasing your giving). Possibilities might include giving to a faith community, overseas development and humanitarian work, work amongst the disadvantaged in Australia, Christian mission

work, ecological conservation and restoration, or a campaign for justice.

- Explore pooling your giving (or a portion of your giving) with others to fund some innovative work in your local area or within your faith community.
- Commit to keeping your eyes open for a person for whom a financial gift (even a small one) might be a help or an encouragement. Think about how you could make such a gift anonymously.

6. Savings & Investment
The building up of one another

What's the Problem?

We are continually told that 'your money should be working for you'. Indeed, for many, this is not only smart advice, it is the essence of being *responsible*. Having well-invested money is part of being a good parent and a good citizen and, some would even say, a good Christian. It is revealing that, for many modern Christians, 'good investment' is synonymous with 'good stewardship'.

This way of thinking is so ubiquitous, so seemingly self-evident, so *moralistic*, that we hardly stop to inquire more deeply into what is being said. If money is able to earn more money without our labour, how does it do it? Of course, the answer is simple: through a savings account, an investment portfolio or a real estate investment. But what are these magical things that simply take our money and make more money? How do they do it? If they are able to generate a return on investment, where does the increase come from? It is these simple questions we need to be asking if we are to truly take care for the impact we are having in the world.

When thinking about savings and investment, we are thinking about anything that produces a return without your labour: savings accounts and term deposits, superannuation funds, stocks, shares and bonds, and real estate. Of these, real estate is the most direct and tangible form of investment, with the individual investor usually driving all the key decisions; we shall consider this form of investment later. The other three kinds of investment form part of that rarefied and mysterious world of finance. These 'financial products' are a familiar part of everyday life and yet very few people have much of an understanding of what they actually are and do. So where does the return come from?

At its most basic level, whenever you put money into a bank, you are *lending* them your money with the understanding that they can use those funds to go out and make as much money as they like, as long as they pay you back an agreed amount of interest on top of your principal. Traditionally, the bank would simply do this by lending out the money that you (and others) lend them - usually for a business loan or home loan - to someone else at a higher interest rate. In effect, you are making your money from the loan paid to the other person and the bank makes its money on the difference between the two: the interest rates. At the time of writing, my bank is offering 2.2 per cent interest for term deposits and charging 3.99 per cent for home loans.

However, over the last 30 years, banks - especially the large ones- have diversified their investments into the much more complex realm of *global finance*. This is the obscure world of the stock market, currency trading, bonds, securities and other financial derivatives, which are so complex that hardly anyone understands them. Since the 1990s and the beginning of compulsory superannuation, the retirement savings of most Australians (and many others around the world) have also been staked to the fortunes of global finance. Indeed, superannuation funds have emerged as one of the big players in a very big game.

The most visible part of the finance world is the stock market, where company shares are bought and sold. Once the exclusive territory of businessmen, the buying and selling of shares has increasingly become normalised for 'Mum and Dad investors', especially those on higher incomes. Buying shares in a company makes you a part-owner of that company, entitling you to a share of its profits and giving you a say in how it is run. Moreover (and this is where the real interest in share ownership lies), if a company is doing well, then the value of its shares rise, which means that if you can sell shares for a higher price than you bought them, you stand to make a windfall profit. In theory, shareholding should mean that share owners have a stake in ensuring that a company is well run *and* profitable. However, in reality, the primary interest in shareholding has been in the rising value of shares and companies have often been run according to this overriding concern.

Which company shares are most attractive to investors? Clearly, those from companies that make the largest profits. How do you make large profits? Ah, there's the rub. We would like to think companies are profitable because they provide a good service or a good product for their customers. This can be true, but unfortunately there are also many less noble ways a company can extract profit. Two of the primary ways are to pay as little as possible for the resources they extract from the earth and pay as little as possible for the labour they extract from workers. We see this clearly in the operation of the global mining industry in developing countries, where vast profits have been made digging up gold, silver, copper and other minerals, yet so often local landscapes and ecologies are left devastated. This is yet another blow to biodiversity (see chapter 4) and often severely adversely affects local communities who are dependent on the rivers, farming land and forests that have been destroyed. In developing countries, the true cost of this damage to the environment and the loss of local livelihoods is very rarely compensated adequately.

The operation of the global textile industry provides a clear example of companies seeking to locate their production in countries where they can pay the least for labour. This can exert pressure on governments in those countries to keep their labour standards weak and minimum wages low so as to entice multinational investors; a clear factor in the failures that led to the tragic collapse of the Rana Plaza garment factory in Bangladesh in 2013, killing more than 1100 people.

Mining and textiles are two well-known and easy examples of the ways in which profit can be made from underpaying the *true* costs of production. However, there are thousands more. This is not to say that all profitable companies behave in this way, but such behaviour is widespread among companies listed on the stock exchange. When our money goes into a bank or superannuation fund, it is into this world that it is invested. The return, which we see simply as a percentage rate, has a very real (albeit complex) story of people and places behind it.

It is not an exaggeration to say that finance now rules the world. Since the 1970s, the floating of the world's currencies and financial deregulation have combined to produce a remarkable growth in the global finance sector. Since the 1990s, compulsory superannuation and the rise of superannuation funds have provided a massive source of new investment for the finance industry. Today, the size of the financial derivatives market dwarfs the real-world economy by a factor of at least 10:1. Whereas the total value of all goods and services bought and sold around the world each year was around US$107 trillion (2014), the size of *finance* trading was thought to be around US$1,200 trillion, or US $1.2 *quadrillion*. That means less than ten per cent of the money that zips electronically around the world each day is actually being used to buy things; most of it is being used simply to make more money.

Although the financial economy is in many ways detached from the real-world economy, it still has the power to completely dominate the economic decisions of world governments. We saw this in 2008, when the trading activity of a frighteningly small number of people brought the world to its knees, forcing world governments into an economic bailout whose total price tag – that is, the cost to taxpayers - approached US$14-15 trillion. This, in turn, forced governments everywhere to adopt austerity budgets, slashing spending on health care, education, welfare, foreign aid, humanitarian assistance and refugee intake. When the super-elite world of finance sneezes, it is the poor who catch a cold.

However, the human impact of the global financial crisis was much less than that of another far less well-known crisis that took place the same year: the 2008 food crisis. That year, the price of grains spiked around the world, doubling on average, suddenly making food unaffordable for a large number of the world's poor. In 2008, there were food riots in 30 countries across three continents. According to the UN's Food and Agriculture Organisation, an *additional* 75 million people went hungry that year. The causes of the food crisis were multiple and complex. However, one factor that increased its severity, especially impacting the price of wheat, was the role of finance. In late 2007, as the sub-prime mortgage crisis began to bite in the US, the big pension and superannuation funds all began to withdraw their money from real estate and look for a more profitable sector. They began speculating in food futures markets, bidding up the price of wheat in a mad auction whose end result was a lot of hungry people. There was never actually a shortage of wheat in 2008.

What connection do we have to this strange and rarefied economy? Quite simply, if you have money in a term deposit with a major bank or if you have a standard superannuation fund and that is the vast majority of adult Australians - then your money is being used in all of these things. If you had money in a standard superannuation fund in 2008, there is a good chance that you unwittingly profited from the misery of the food crisis.

What about buying an investment property? This is a much more direct and tangible form of investment, usually under the direct control of the person investing the money. And surely it also provides a needed service - a rental home - for the community? Generally, this is true. However, there are a number of complicating factors, meaning that real estate investment has become associated with some quite negative impacts on society. The most prominent of these is, of course, the housing affordability crisis that has gripped much of the developed world.

In 2011, a US-based survey of international housing affordability has pointed out that Australia, 'once the exemplar of modestly priced, high-quality middle-class housing' has now become 'the most unaffordable housing market in the English-speaking world'. While around 51 per cent of homes sold in Australia in 2004 were affordable to 'moderate income-earners', this had slipped to just 28 per cent by 2012. The situation is even worse for those on low incomes looking for rental properties: in 2014, less than one per cent of rental properties advertised were affordable for anyone on a government payment. Those with complex needs, such as single parents and people with a disability, are experiencing even greater difficulty finding rental properties.

What has happened? Since the 1990s, housing has increasingly been viewed by governments and citizens alike as a source of wealth accumulation. Encouraged by tax incentives such as negative gearing and lowering of the capital gains tax, investors have aggressively entered the housing market, buying and selling to take advantage of rising prices, all the while bidding up the cost of housing. Put simply, the reason why housing in Australia is so ridiculously unaffordable is that houses have become the prime arena for profit-taking in the midst of a widespread culture of greed. Governments have encouraged this and 'Mum and Dad' investors have been all-too-willing participants.

What Does the Bible Say?

The world of global finance is a universe away from the world of the Old Testament. Nonetheless, even in those ancient times there was a strong comprehension that capital could all-too-easily be put to uses that were destructive, so it is perhaps not surprising that some of the Bible's strongest teachings on economic ethics concern the ethics of credit - what we would today call 'investment'.

A central pillar of Old Testament economic ethics was the prohibition on charging interest on a loan to a countryman. To us, for whom the charging of interest is an unquestioned fact of daily life, this comes as quite a shock. However, the language is quite insistent, and it is worth quoting the first appearance of this instruction at length:

> You shall not wrong or oppress a resident alien, for you were aliens in the land of Egypt. You shall not abuse any widow or orphan. If you do abuse them, when they cry out to me, I will surely heed their cry; my wrath will burn, and I will kill you with the sword, and your wives shall become widows and your children orphans. *If you lend money to my people, to the poor among you, you shall not deal with them as a creditor; you shall not exact interest from them.* If you take your neighbour's cloak in pawn, you shall restore it before the sun goes down; for it may be your neighbour's only clothing to use as

cover; in what else shall that person sleep? And if your neighbour cries out to me, I will listen, for I am compassionate. (Ex 22:21-27)

In this passage, the precursor to the instruction about interest is a very strong injunction to do right by the poor and marginalised, and it is framed by recalling the Israelites to their own liberation from slavery in Egypt (an exploration of the relationship between debt and slavery is in the next chapter). In this context, the charging of interest on a loan was seen as a core injustice and it is extended to the taking of collateral in pledge for the loan. This teaching is repeated in Leviticus (25:35-37) and Deuteronomy (23:19-20).

It needs to be pointed out that the lending being discussed here is not business loans, but lending to people in need, such as in the case of a failed crop or the sickness of one of the main workers in the household. These generally would not even have been loans of money but food, usually grain. The very simple ethic, then, at the heart of the Old Testament teaching on charging interest was a horror that some people might grow their own wealth (via interest on a loan) by exploiting *someone else's need*. Moreover, to the ancient mind, the idea that one could grow one's own wealth without actually doing anything, but merely by the fact of having accumulated wealth, seemed to be a violation of natural justice. The repugnance of this is so strong that in Deuteronomy the teaching prohibiting interest is listed among associated teachings on wet dreams, faeces, slavery and prostitution (Deut 23:9-25).

It has long been forgotten by Western Christians that for the first 1500 years of Christian history the church also forbade the charging of interest on loans. It wasn't until the Protestant Reformation that Calvin began to make allowances for charging interest (Luther was implacably opposed to it). In the midst of a more commercially sophisticated urban economy, Calvin could see the need to make a distinction between those borrowing to consume in a time of need and those borrowing to invest in a commercial venture; charging interest on the first was still prohibited, but it was permitted for the latter. Even then, Calvin put such tight strictures on the charging of interest that much of what is considered normal today would not have been permitted.

In the Old Testament, the teachings on lending only applied to one's own people; charging interest was permitted when lending to a foreigner. Such people were both strangers (and, therefore, more risky to lend to), and also were not considered part of the Israelite community of right relationship. However, when we get to the gospels, Jesus urges his followers to go well beyond the stipulations of the Hebrew law around interest; Jesus asks his followers to lend to their *enemies* and to lend *without expecting repayment*:

> If you lend to those from whom you hope to receive, what credit is that to you? Even sinners lend to sinners, to receive as much again. But love your enemies, do good, and lend, expecting nothing in return. (Lk 6:34-35)

Characteristically, this is yet another of Jesus' teachings on money that seem designed to give accountants and financial planners heart palpitations. Indeed, Jesus seems to advocate what many would piously denounce as 'bad stewardship'. Why?

Perhaps one of the hardest things for us to get our heads around, and one of the most challenging things for us to accept, is that Jesus basically rejects the whole premise of the modern conception of 'savings and investment', which is *accumulation*. We will get to how we practically wrestle with this in the section below, but it is important we are clear about what Jesus actually taught.

Jesus' teachings on accumulation - 'growing your nest egg' - are clear and direct:

> Do not store up for yourselves treasures on earth, where moth and rust consume and where thieves break in and steal; but store up for yourselves treasures in heaven, where neither moth nor rust consumes and where thieves do not break in and steal. For where your treasure is, there your heart will be also. (Mt 6:19-21)

It seems clear enough that Jesus completely rejects seeking greater wealth and comfort - what we would call a 'higher standard of living' - as a life goal. It is a spiritual law that the more material wealth we have, the more we have *invested* in that wealth, to the detriment of other concerns. More than that, Jesus saw the goal of accumulation as positively perilous to spiritual health: 'what will it profit them to gain the whole world and forfeit their life?' (Mk 8:36). He says of the rich man who is building bigger barns for his wealth: 'You fool! This very night your life will be demanded of you.' (Lk 12:20, NIV).

Perhaps even more confronting is that Jesus also challenges accumulation for the sake of *security*. Only a few verses after he says 'Do not store up treasures for yourselves' in the Sermon on the Mount, he says:

> I tell you, do not worry about your life, what you will eat or what you will drink, or about your body, what you will wear. [...] For it is the Gentiles who strive for all these things; and indeed your heavenly Father knows that you need all these things. But strive first for the kingdom of God and his righteousness, and all these things will be given to you as well. So do not worry about tomorrow, for tomorrow will bring worries of its own. Today's trouble is enough for today. (Mt 6:25-34)

There is a great deal in this teaching that requires unpacking and more than can be accomplished here. For our purposes, though, it is enough to simply recognise that what Jesus is calling us to here is *a profound re-ordering of our material priorities*. Whereas our natural inclination is to invest our money and mental energy in securing our future (or, more accurately, what we *imagine* will secure our future), Jesus is encouraging us to invest ourselves - and for him it is always our *whole* selves (time, money, mental energy) - in the kingdom of God.

Overall, there is very little in Jesus' teachings on money and possessions, and those of the rest of the New Testament, that can be reconciled with the modern culture of 'making your money work for you'. His teachings are difficult, but clear and consistent. However, there is one passage of the gospels that has confused this clarity somewhat, and that is the so-called 'stewardship parables': the Parable of the Talents in Matthew (Mt 25:14-30) and the Parable of the Minas in Luke (Lk 19:11-27).[1]

For the last few hundred years, the Stewardship Parables have been consistently used by Christians who wish to argue that shrewd investment of money (that is, getting a good return) represents 'good stewardship' and is a Christian obligation. The claim is that, in these parables, Jesus is commending lending with interest and very high rates of interest at that. However, this is actually a gross misreading. An interpretation that is truer to the stories themselves (most clearly in the case of Luke's story) and consistent with everything else Jesus has said in the gospels (for both Matthew and Luke) leads us to the reverse conclusion of what has become the mainstream exegesis of these texts.

To demonstrate this properly requires going into the texts in some detail, which cannot be done here, but it is such an important misreading of the Bible to correct that I have included a longer discussion on the subject in the appendices of this book. Here, let me briefly outline the main points of the argument:

1. The Parable of the Talents (Matthew) and the Parable of the Minas (Luke) are essentially the same story; however, they differ in some important ways. Matthew's story is enigmatic and poses some tricky questions for interpretation, whichever way you read it. However, Luke's story is resoundingly clear and unambiguous. Where there is uncertainty over how to read Matthew, we should be guided by Luke's clarity.

2. These are not introduced as kingdom parables – they do not tell us about God and how he works. They are stories about something else.

3. The signals about the king and the two servants who profitably invest the money are overwhelmingly *negative* signals, caricaturing the *opposite* of the kingdom that Jesus had been talking about. In particular, *a high return on investment is directly associated with injustice and oppression.*

---

1 In some translations 'minas' is translated as 'pounds'.

4. The third servant – the one who is generally considered the bad guy - is the one who refuses to engage in injustice and speaks truth to power, for which he pays the price. This is exactly what will happen to Jesus (in Luke's version this actually provides the context and the reason for the story!).

5. The clincher: to imagine that Jesus, in these two parables, is commending lucrative investment of money requires us to ignore everything else he has taught about money (consistently and powerfully) in the rest of the gospels.

The upshot is that, once read more carefully, these stories - especially Luke's version – provide the most searing indictment of high-yielding financial investment that can be found in the gospels.

How Might We Respond?

There is a marked divide between how different households approach savings and investment. For some households, giving thought to savings and investment will seem irrelevant, as their finances are completely tied up in week-to-week consumption and paying off debt (see next chapter). For others, great energy and attention will have been given to organising family finances around growing a nest-egg. Nevertheless, the reality is that these days most Australian households are de facto shareholders through compulsory superannuation and most households will seek to save at some point in their life cycle, so it is important that everyone gives some thought to where their money is and what it is doing in the world.

The teaching of Jesus around finances is so radically different to our deeply held cultural attitudes that modern Christians have generally found it convenient to ignore them altogether. However, just because we are not able to follow these teachings *literally* – who can honestly live up to 'do not worry about tomorrow'? - does not mean we should not still try to take them *very seriously*. As with all biblical instruction, we need to be asking ourselves what principle is at stake and what the purposes of God may be in challenging us this way.

Whether or not to save

The hardest task in thinking through this area of household economics is the spiritual task of opening up our deep-seated financial fears and desires to challenge. If we are involved in saving and investing our money, what is driving our decisions? By now it should be clear that investing for the purposes of expanding our already opulent standards of living - a goal that is generally considered normal - is clearly rejected by Jesus as a goal that leads us away from 'the life that really is life' and something that implicates us deeply in economic injustice.

Is Jesus really against all forms of saving? Perhaps it will come as some relief to know that the church, even from its earliest days, has never taken Jesus' instructions 'Do not store up treasures' or 'Do not worry about tomorrow' as a literal command against any form of saving. However, it is very clear that the strength of Jesus' language is precisely intended to severely shake up the cultural attitudes that shape us.

To the extent that saving represents a discipline of living within your means - actually, *below* your means - it is something to be commended. In a culture of consumer gratification (see chapter 2) and living beyond your means (see chapter 6), the discipline of saving plays a positive restraining role. However, if we have money that is surplus to our needs, we first need to make a choice between *saving* for ourselves or *giving* to others (see chapter 4). Here we have, in the most practical way, an example of the perpetual spiritual struggle to die to self and move in compassion towards the other. This does not imply, by any means, that giving should always trump saving; it should at least be clear, however, that following Jesus requires us to locate the balance between the two quite differently to where our cultural programming would have it.

The question then arises: saving for what? Surely if we have a worthy goal - a deposit for a house, building a shed, a special journey or holiday - it is far better to follow the discipline of waiting, working and saving then to go into debt. The spiritual/ethical question here is simply whether the goal we are pursuing is worth the investment of time, money and energy that it represents. In this picture, a deposit for a house stacks up differently from an overseas holiday.

What about where the goal is simply saving (or investing) for security in one's old age? This is an enormously difficult question, as how we answer it depends on a complex mix of ingredients. Family context is critical: those with cohesive well-functioning families will generally feel more intrinsically secure that there will be someone to take care of them in old age than someone whose family is fragmented and alienated from one another, or someone who has no real family. Such people will understandably feel that having some money put away will give them more security. Nevertheless, whatever one's family context, there is a point where healthy prudence becomes an unhealthy fear of the unknown. Where is this point? It is not for me to say, but if we are not aware that such a point exists, and if we have never at least wrestled with whether our prudence has become fear, then we are likely to fall into that trap.

At the heart of this all is the deeper matter of trust in God. This is itself a very difficult matter, as at one level we simply must reject any simplistic formulation that 'if you trust God everything will be alright'. The New Testament is quite clear that Christians could experience need and deprivation and should probably even expect to at some stage. On the other hand, the whole thrust of the Bible is to call us into a faith in which our fundamental sense of security and contentment is secure *whatever* our material circumstances.

Moreover, it needs to be stressed that the question of security in old age is also a function of our *expectations* about standards of living. There is not much question in 21st century Australia about going without the basics of food and shelter, so the real question is *how much* do we consider to be adequate? The higher we set this bar, the harder the task of ensuring that we are 'secure'; the lower our expectations about standard of living, the more 'secure' we become.

Superannuation

To some extent, questions about saving and security have become a moot point, as the institution of compulsory superannuation already forces workers to save and invest to secure their retirement. From a policy perspective, this is a sensible response by government to the challenge of an inverting age pyramid and the prospect of a ballooning pension bill. However, as we have seen, from an individual Christian perspective it raises some ethical challenges due to ways in which superannuation funds invest their massive pools of money. The question, then, is whether there are ways in which we can ensure that our super investments do no harm in the world, or, more positively, whether they can actually be directed to supporting beneficial work.

What is superannuation? Quite simply, it is a means of forced saving in which regular contributions from workers are pooled together in large 'funds' which are then invested on our behalf with the view to ensuring a good return. Superannuation funds generally invest across a number of areas - company shares, bonds, property and that strange world of 'finance' - with the mix determined by the balance of risk versus return. Generally speaking, the level of risk versus (hoped-for) return is the only thing you get to choose when it comes to how your super is invested; everything else is done at multiple arms-length from your control.

As we have seen, this system means that superannuation implicates us all in some of the worst behaviour of the finance market, whether turning us into defacto owners of mining companies that have an appalling ecological and social justice record in developing countries, or speculation on commodities markets or playing games with currency fluctuations. What can we do?

Since 2005, most Australian employees have had the legal right to *choose* their superannuation fund. The best option available to most people is to choose an *ethical superannuation fund*. What does this mean?

Ideas about ethical investment, or socially responsible investment, have been around since the time of the anti-slave trade movement in the 18th century. In the last few decades, these have been systematised into standards and best practice approaches. At its most basic, an ethical investment fund uses a 'negative screen' to rule out investing in harmful sectors such as tobacco, weapons, gambling, coal mining, old forest logging and potentially a range of other areas. The better ethical investment funds will also use 'positive screen', which means they prioritise investment in sectors that are considered broadly beneficial, such as renewable energy, sustainable agriculture, community infrastructure, efficient technology, and so on. The best ethical investment funds will also screen individual companies according to their record around things such as environmental sustainability, labour rights and animal exploitation. All good ethical investment funds should provide transparent and easy-to-access information about the exact nature of their negative and positive screens, and exactly which companies they have invested in over the last few years.

In Australia there is a range of ethical investment funds on offer with varying quality, so it is probably best to choose one that has been accredited by an independent peak body, such as the Responsible Investment Association Australasia (RIAA).[2] No ethical superannuation fund, whether accredited or not, is perfect or will invest entirely according to your ethical preferences; they do, however, represent *the best option available*. Interestingly, ethical super funds have, on average, provided higher returns than the sector as a whole.

Finally, for a very few people, there is the option of self-managed superannuation, which allows you a much higher level of control (although not complete control) over how your superannuation money is invested. However, this really only makes sense if you have quite considerable sums of money to invest and also have a high level of financial skills and the requisite time and energy it needs. Anyone considering this course should talk to a financial adviser, preferably one that has been accredited by the Responsible Investment Association.

Banks and financial institutions

Banks or financial institutions play an essential and very useful role in the day-to-day operations of the monetary economy and it is virtually impossible to get by in modern society without one. However, as we have seen, banks and financial institutions are also implicated in a global financial economy that is profoundly corrosive. Recognising

---

2 Search: 'Responsible Investment Association Australasia'. At the time of writing, there were eight accredited ethical super funds.

our ongoing need of financial institutions, what choices can we make to limit our participation in the worst elements of this world?

Firstly, it is helpful to recognise the distinctions between different sorts of financial institutions. While there are none that are free of any ethical concerns, there are certainly some sorts that provide a more constructive service at a human level and are less involved in destructive processes at a global level.

In Australia, the 'big four' banks - NAB, Commonwealth Bank, Westpac and ANZ - are all highly enmeshed in the world of global finance with all its harms and injustices, whether it is in currency and commodity speculation, investment in fossil fuels, or projects in the developing world that are guilty of human rights violations and ecological destruction. Moreover, as the 2018 Banking Royal Commission amply demonstrated, each of the 'big four' have a very poor record of ethical dealing with customers and communities, whether it is questionable lending practices, aggressive foreclosing of loans or closing branches and shedding staff in towns and smaller centres, all the while making immense profits.

By contrast, credit unions have much less exposure to the world of global finance and they are more enmeshed in local communities. Historically, credit unions, along with friendly societies and mutual societies, arose as ventures in cooperative community finance to serve segments of the community, often working class, who had no access to financial institutions. They allowed working people to pool their savings and thus gain access to loans at non-usurious rates.

Today, credit unions have developed significantly from these humble roots. However, they remain distinct from the big banks in two important ways: (i) they are *member-owned institutions*, which means they exist to benefit their 'customers', who are also the owners, and not absentee shareholders who demand continually higher profits and dividends; and (ii) most of the money deposited in credit unions is recycled as home loans and personal loans to members - not invested in some military-owned gas pipeline in Burma or speculation on the Boston futures market in wheat. Credit unions tend to have much higher levels of customer service and tend to have more responsible lending practices.

In recent times, some credit unions, have grown into 'banks' - Bank Australia and Members Equity Bank (ME Bank) - which means they come under different regulatory rules, however, they generally retain the same core attributes described above. Some of these have an impressive record in socially and ecologically responsible investing. Similarly, the Community Bank branches of the Bendigo Bank are effectively locally owned banks that provide impressive local service and cycle money through their own communities.

In short, if you are interested in limiting the harm your money does in the world and increasing the chance it may be used in beneficial ways, the choice is simple: move your money out of the 'big four' banks and into a credit union or member-owned bank.

Investment properties

Depending on how it is done, investing in property can be either the most directly beneficial or the most directly exploitative form of investment. In recent times, large numbers of people have entered the market for investment properties tempted by the lure of high returns. However, it is these high returns for property investors that, looked at from the other side, represent the facts of the housing affordability crisis for home buyers and renters.

If buying an investment property is not to be an exploitative form of parasitism, then it must be undertaken from a completely different basis. First and foremost, the goal of *maximising your return* must be jettisoned. The logic of profit maximisation leads to a more rapid turnover of buying and selling properties, always seeking the highest bidder, and to pushing rents up to the limit the market will bear. These are the engine of the housing affordability crisis. The only responsible way to invest in property is to be happy to accept lower returns than are generally sought.

Secondly, the language of 'property' and 'real estate' must be jettisoned and replaced by the consciousness that the things being bought, sold and let out are *homes*. Homes are a basic need of humans and they are the basis of wellbeing and health for families. Becoming clear about this - the human implications of owning someone else's home - sheds a whole new light on the responsibilities and obligations of investing in housing. If this act can be done not only with thought for 'return', but also with the goal of service, then it opens up a whole new possibility for the social character of investing.

Practically, this means rethinking all of the key decisions of 'property investing' from a different basis:

1. What sort of property to buy? What sort of housing is most needed?

2. The level of rent that is charged: rather than determine what you *could* get, set the rent by what your needs, modestly determined, are.

3. The level of service and maintenance that is provided: rather than try to keep these 'costs' at an absolute minimum, ask what is needed to provide a decent home. This includes questions of sustainability: is the house insulated and draft-proofed or will tenants need to rack up large bills on heating and cooling, with the accompanying greenhouse gases, just to be comfortable?

4. Choosing a real estate agent: there is a great deal of variability in the ways real estate agents treat renters and every agent will push for rents to be as high as the market will bear (they receive a commission). In Melbourne, there is a not-for-profit real estate agent (Home Ground) whose core purpose is to end homelessness and therefore acts quite differently from conventional real estate agencies. Whatever the case, if property investing is to be broadly beneficial it requires taking responsibility for the behaviour of the people who are acting as your agents or consider abandoning using an agent altogether.

A new way of thinking about investment

Finally, for those few people who do find themselves with large amounts of surplus money (perhaps after receiving an inheritance) and wondering what to do with it, it is worth re-thinking the purpose and meaning of 'investment'. If we put a lot of time and energy into supporting a person or group, we often say 'I really *invested* in that (person/group)', by which we mean we gave something of ourselves for the building up of another. This is the essential attitude that Paul encourages the Christian community to pursue in relation to each other: 'So then, let us pursue the things which make for peace and the building up of one another' (Rom 14:19, NAS). Imagine if we applied this thinking not only to our spiritual gifts, but also to our financial 'gifts'. Imagine if the fundamental premise for thinking about 'investment' was not the question 'What return can I get?' but rather, 'What good purpose can I support with this money?' This does not necessarily mean that all thought of return must be jettisoned (although this becomes one possibility), but it does suggest subordinating return to larger concerns and being prepared to accept lower returns than would be possible on the open market.

Beginning from this basis could lead in a number of different directions. It could lead into buying an 'investment property' with the purpose of providing affordable and secure housing to people in your community who are struggling with housing, or to explore ethical investing, or to some more creative ventures in 'community investing'. This could include providing low interest loans or no interest loans to members of your community seeking to buy a home or start a business, or to a small Christian ministry that is getting underway.

Things become even more interesting when you move beyond thinking about investment individually and start to think cooperatively. In many churches, there is a mix of capital-rich and capital-poor members and some of the latter category will be struggling with housing. Imagine what might be possible if those capital-rich members chose to pool their money to start some form of cooperative credit to support members of their church community, or creative initiatives

129

in the broader community, or both. Such possibilities suggest that the church has a real need for kingdom-minded accountants: people who understand the complexities and possibilities of money - the devil in the detail - but who also understand the radically different ethic of money that is called forth by the gospel.

Examples of steps people have taken

- Simply seek to educate yourself on 'ethical', 'responsible' and 'community' investing.
- Move all your superannuation into an 'ethical super' fund. To research ethical super, see http://www.responsibleinvestment.org
- Switch any savings or term deposits from one of the 'Big 4' banks (Westpac, Commonwealth, NAB, ANZ) into a credit union or member-owned bank.
- Do you have money in investment funds or share portfolios? Explore moving this money into ethical funds or out of the share market altogether.
- Do you own an investment property? What would it take to transform this investment into a service meeting a human need (especially for people in need of housing) rather than just an investment maximised for financial benefit? Consider:
  - what rent is fair (rather than what the market allows you to charge)?
  - what relationship or connection do you have with the tenants?
  - can you dispense with using a real estate agent to 'manage' the tenancy of your property?
- Consider direct person-to-person loans. Are there any in your church or community who could benefit from a no interest or low interest loan?

7. DEBT
Freedom to follow God

What's the Problem?

It is hard to overemphasise the extent to which the modern attitude to debt has undergone a revolution. Whereas once the primary concern of household finances was how to ensure saving, now the primary concern is debt obligations. Debt was once a matter of gravity; now it is ubiquitous and entered into with little thought. Debt is now as much a part of the landscape of everyday household economics as groceries. Indeed, many households use debt to buy groceries.

Since the end of the 1980s, Australians have engaged in an orgy of borrowing. Household debt quadrupled between 1988 and 2015 and debt levels grew at a rate four times faster than growth in income. Whereas in 1988 the average household debt was 64 per cent of income, by 2015 that had risen to 185 per cent of income. In 2015, Australian households were amongst the most indebted on earth, and this at a time when Australian incomes were higher than ever before. In 2015, the net worth of the average Australian adult was second only to Switzerland.

There are a number of reasons for this explosion of debt. The largest component of household debt is due to the boom of property prices (see chapter 5), forcing prospective home buyers into ever-larger mortgages. In the 20 years between 1995 and 2015, the average home loan increased from $95,000 to $387,000. The median house price in Melbourne in 2015 generally required a salary of over $100,000 in order to meet mortgage repayments.

To some extent, home buyers, and especially first home buyers, have been the victims of a greed-fuelled real estate investment frenzy. However, another contributing factor to the growing size of housing debt are the *ballooning expectations* about the size and quality of home that people feel will be adequate. The average size of a new Australian house increased by 40 per cent between 1984 and 2003, from 162 square metres to 227 square metres. Since the turn of the century, Australians have been building the largest new houses in the world. On average, Australians now occupy twice as much floor space as their grandparents did. Not only does this demand for larger houses increase the amount of energy and water we consume (see chapter 3), it also increases the debt load of Australian families.

While housing debt is by far the largest portion of the debt pie, it has perhaps been the role of credit cards that has done the most to revolutionise attitudes towards debt. Credit cards have their origins in the 1920s with the beginning of store credit at the large department stores; however, it was the refinement of the technology of plastic bank cards that perhaps did the most to transform attitudes to consumer credit. In Australia, this took place in the 1970s and has been credited by some as issuing in the age of modern consumerism.

Use of credit cards accelerated dramatically from the turn of the century and was not particularly affected by the global financial crisis. In the ten years between 2004 and 2014, the number of accounts, the number of transactions and the size of transactions all rose steeply. That is, more people were spending more money more often on their credit cards. In this period, credit card debt in Australia grew by 88 per cent. By 2015, the average Australian adult had two credit cards with a credit limit of $9,000 per card and roughly half of Australian households were using credit cards to pay bills. The average credit card holder in Australia had a credit card debt of $4,300 (not counting debt where no interest is being charged). While two-thirds of Australians reported that they paid off their cards before they attracted interest, banks reported that two-thirds of accounts were attracting interest.

It is hard to exaggerate the role credit cards have played in shaping the modern consumer mentality. They have affected the overthrow of the ethos of 'save to buy' and replaced it with the lure of 'buy now, pay later'. The consumption binge we have witnessed since the 1990s (see chapter 2) is critically linked to a new demand for instant gratification that has, in large part, been facilitated by credit cards. Moreover, credit cards have released households (at least temporarily) from the age-old constraint of needing to discipline their finances so that income and expenditure are kept in balance. In the age of easy credit, it has become possible to live beyond your means for an extended period of time. Indeed, there is reportedly now a sub-stratum of credit card users whose only aim is to be able to afford the minimum repayment each month and whose debt is so huge it will likely never be paid off.

Perhaps even more disturbing was the insidious growth of payday lending during this period. These are small loans at high interest rates, with little or no eligibility criteria. This form of credit targets low-income people – generally the welfare-dependent – who are struggling to pay household bills. Loans may be from a couple of hundred dollars to a couple of thousand; however, the interest rates, charged monthly, can amount to as much as 240 per cent per year. It is not surprising that people who use payday lenders often end up in a debt spiral. One study found that two-thirds of the customers of payday lenders had taken out more than one loan in a short period of time, often borrowing to pay off previous loans. Between 2008 and 2014, payday lending grew by 125 per cent.

An obvious impact of this growing debt burden on families is stress. A study in 2015 found that one-quarter of households were experiencing financial stress. Not surprisingly, welfare-dependent households had the highest rates of financial stress (67 per cent). However, alarmingly, more than a quarter of middle-income households (families with incomes of $70k - $110k p.a.) reported the same. This has real implications for the health of families, as such stress is often an aggravating factor in family breakdown.

Another impact of growing debt is vulnerability. As many economists have worriedly pointed out, households have taken on large debts in a period of historically low interest rates when it seems that the repayments of such debt are affordable. However, should interest rates begin to return to levels more commonly seen, then a very large number of households will struggle to make repayments. At a global level, the relationship between international finance and household debt remains a major vulnerability of the economic system as a whole. It was the widespread defaulting on home mortgages in America that began the global financial crisis in 2007 and, alarmingly, little has been done to improve the financial system's exposure to such threats.

Finally, a little-considered impact of debt is the loss of freedom. A debt is, by definition, an obligation to someone else. The increased debt of families is an increase of their obligations to a financial institution, underpinned by the force of law. This means two things: (i) it increases pressure on those families to produce a certain income; (ii) it limits the range of life choices they can make, most notably the major choices they can make about time. That is, debt has a tendency to propel people beyond their initial intention into a form of living – time-poor, fast consumption – which they may have only half-chosen.

In summary, we can see that the culture of debt-driven consumerism has widespread and deep impacts. Our unsustainable exploitation of the planet, with all its concomitant impacts upon the poor (see chapters 2 and 3), is intimately connected with the ways in which debt has allowed us to live beyond our means financially. Moreover, despite incomes being higher than ever before, the increased debt load of households is likely a major factor behind their lack of financial generosity (see chapter 4). And, of course, the increased debt load of households, which is an increased obligation of financial repayments, mandates that families must attract a certain amount of income, and that has a determinative impact on how they think about employment and time, with a resulting impact on the place that relationships and non-income-earning pursuits have in life (see chapter 1). Finally, all this debt has only been made possible by a global financial system that is perverse, exploitative and unstable (see chapter 5).

What Does the Bible Say?

Debt is a subject of major significance in the Bible. Biblical texts are concerned about both the socio-economic effects of debt and its theological implications. In the Old Testament, debt is viewed as a necessary evil, but one that requires strict bounds around it. The starting point of the various instructions about debt contained within the Torah is the realistic assumption that, for one reason or another, there will always be a need for some people to borrow from others. In the ancient agrarian world, the primary reason for this was the failure of a crop or some similar misfortune; but whatever the circumstances, there is a recognition that borrowing is a legitimate response to *need*. To this end, there is even a commendation in Deuteronomy to lend to those in need (Deut 15:7-11).

However, in the ancient world, as today, the position of indebtedness was a vulnerable one. There was always the danger that debt could become a downward spiral into poverty and dependence. The existence of such poverty traps leads inexorably to a widening gap between rich and poor in a society and the whole vision of the Promised Land was that none would have too little and none would have too much. Moreover, for ancients, the end point of the debt spiral was not bankruptcy, it was *slavery*. In Israel, as in the rest of the ancient world, the final means to settle an unpaid debt was to enter the household of the creditor and to work for them in a form of slavery known as debt bondage.

It is this close correspondence between debt and slavery that makes debt a major subject of concern in the Bible. The central act in Israel's salvation history was their liberation by God from slavery in Egypt, so it was intolerable that Israelites would begin enslaving each other. The teachings on debt in Deuteronomy and Leviticus are explicit on this point: 'Remember that you were a slave in the land of Egypt, and the Lord your God redeemed you; for this reason I lay this command upon you today' (Deut 15:15).

It is important to understand that God's desire for the Israelites to be free from slavery extends deeper than just a concern for social justice, although it is clearly also that. The whole meaning of the liberation from Egypt was not just that they would be free, but that they would be *free to follow God*. Again and again, the refrain of the Torah is that God is *calling* Israel to be his people. They are to be 'a priestly kingdom, a holy nation' (Ex 19:6); that is, a people who are to be a witness to God for the rest of the world. However, if God's people are enslaved, whether in Egypt or to each other, then they are not free to follow God and live by his ways – *they have another master*. At the heart of the question of slavery and, by extension, of debt also, is the question of who you are obligated to serve: all debt is entering into an obligation to someone else.

Thus, while the Torah acknowledges that indebtedness would remain a reality, there were a series of mechanisms to limit its harm. The first of these, discussed in the previous chapter, was the prohibition on charging interest. Not only was there a moral horror at the thought of making a profit from someone else's need, prohibiting interest on debts also had the obvious intent of preventing a debt from spiralling out of control. But that was not considered protection enough: the law also required that debts be entirely cancelled every seven years (Deut 15:1-7). It was not unheard of in the ancient world for a new king to cancel debts in celebration of his accession to the throne. However, Israel's king – YHWH – required that cancellation of debts be an ongoing structure of society. In a similar way, anyone who had sold themselves into slavery was to be released every seventh year. When releasing a slave, the former master was to 'provide liberally out of your flock, your threshing floor and your wine press, thus giving to him some of the bounty with which the Lord your God has blessed you.' (Deut 15:14) This was to ensure that a former slave did not enter freedom in destitution and thus in danger of falling back into debt.

Whereas the Deuteronomic laws on debt remission focus on minimising the impact of debt on personal liberty, the Jubilee Laws of Leviticus (Lev 25) go even further, seeking to ensure that debt does not distort the fundamental economic structure of society. Here, the concern was that no family be cut off from the *land*, which was the basic means of production and essential to any family's livelihood, and that this foundational economic good should never be concentrated in the hands of a few. In the event of a family having to sell land to pay a debt, the law provided for a 'right of redemption' by the next-of-kin (25:25-27). This meant that a member of the extended family could step in to buy the land and ensure it did not leave the family and the circle of support this implies. We see a lovely picture of the operation of this law concerning the 'kinsman redeemer' in the story of Ruth and Boaz (Ruth 2:17-21; 4:1-12). If this safeguard failed, there was one more foundational protection against the debt trap: Israelites were to count off 'seven Sabbaths of years' (49 years) and, on the following year, the year of Jubilee, all land was to be returned to its original heritors (Lev 25:8-24). Thus, no family could be permanently alienated from its basic economic sustenance in order pay off debts. In effect, land could not be sold – only a certain number of crops from the land could be sold.

The Jubilee Law envisages a profound and periodic re-booting of economic structures, thus periodically levelling out economic inequality. It is not clear to what extent these laws were ever practised in Israel. What is clear, however, is that *the vision of Jubilee* came to occupy a central place in the biblical vision of a community ordered around right relationship. It is this vision that Jesus famously invokes in Nazareth at the commencement of his ministry in the Gospel of Luke (4:16-19).

When we get to the New Testament, we find that something remarkable has happened to the teaching on debt. At the heart of the Sermon on the Mount are Jesus' instructions about how to pray. It is striking that within this prayer he includes a restatement of the manna economy – 'Give us this day our daily bread' – which is then immediately followed by a restatement of debt remission: 'forgive us our debts, as we also have forgiven our debtors' (Mt 6:12). Only a few verses beforehand, Matthew records Jesus restating the Deuteronomic commendation to lend: 'do not refuse anyone who wants to borrow from you' (Mt 5:42). Here, Jesus seems also to acknowledge both the necessity of debt *and* the undesirability of remaining in the state of indebtedness. However, when we get to further unpacking of the Lord's Prayer, it becomes clear that Jesus has something else in mind as well: 'For if you forgive others their *trespasses*, your heavenly Father will also forgive you; but if you do not forgive others, neither will your Father forgive your *trespasses*' (6:14-15). In Luke's version of the Lord's Prayer, Jesus is recorded as saying 'Forgive us our *sins*, for we ourselves forgive everyone *indebted* to us' (Lk 11:4).

In these striking passages, which are central to the New Testament, the concepts of sin and debt have become blended. Actually, this is not so surprising when you consider that in Aramaic (the language Jesus spoke), unlike Hebrew or Greek, the word for sin and debt is the same word (*ḥōb*). So what did Jesus mean when he said 'Forgive us our debt/ sin as we forgive the debt/sin of others'? Was he talking about spiritual debt or financial debt? As modern readers, we generally want it to be one or the other, but for Jesus and his followers it was probably both.

Sin and debt are like states. I must stress emphatically that this does not mean debt is a sin; remember, Jesus instructs his followers to lend to whoever asks (Mt 5:42). Rather, it means that sin and debt both have an essential quality that is very similar. Sin describes, at root, the introduction of some kind of barrier to a relationship. The barrier may be caused by one, or both parties, having done something harmful or hurtful to the other, or having failed to do something. Either way, sin means there is some outstanding business in a relationship that must be reconciled in order to fully restore that relationship. Such a reconciliation may happen through either some sort of restitution or through forgiveness. This description also describes the state of debt: it is a relationship in which there remains outstanding business that can only be reconciled via repayment or remission. Moreover, sin and debt are also like states in that they are both states of bondage. In John 8, Jesus boldly states, 'everyone who commits sin is a slave to sin' (Jn 8:34), and in Romans 6, the Apostle Paul has an extended discourse on the enslavement of sin.

The amazing news of the gospel is that, in Jesus, God has proclaimed a Jubilee: 'having forgiven us all our transgressions, having cancelled out the certificate of debt consisting of decrees against us and which was hostile to us; and he has taken it out of the way, having nailed it to the cross' (Col 2:14, NASV). It is clear that both Jesus and Paul have taken the Torah vision of Jubilee and debt forgiveness and applied it to a much bigger canvas: that of bondage to sin. Indeed, most of our salvation terminology - 'redemption', 'reconciliation', 'liberation' - are images that relate to debt and slavery. But what does all this mean for what the New Testament taught about actual financial debt?

Compared with the Old Testament, the New Testament's direct guidance about financial debt is scanty. In the world of the New Testament, which is the world of the Roman Empire, any hope of a general societal practice of debt remission had disappeared. For the Gentile hearers and readers of the New Testament, the idea of cancellation of debts was an impossible dream. Nevertheless, as we have seen, it is also clear that the vision of debt cancellation remained instructive for the followers of Jesus. We should not make the mistake of imagining, as has too often been the case, that application of debt language to sin meant that all talk of debt in the New Testament is entirely spiritualised. The fact that Matthew and Luke both retained some reference to forgiveness of debts when they could easily have opted for the word sin (which in Greek is an entirely different word) indicates that financial debt was still very much in view. Luke's rendering ('Forgive us our sins, as we forgive everyone indebted to us') is perhaps suggestive that although the early Christians could not themselves expect to benefit from any broader social structure of debt forgiveness, at least they could forgive other people their debts. This is made explicit in the Sermon on the Plain, where Jesus teaches his followers to 'lend, expecting nothing in return' (Lk 6:35).

But what about teaching concerning their own debt? While there is not much instruction on this, the general understanding seems to be consistent with the Old Testament view that debt is a state of bondage that is best avoided wherever possible. In the Sermon on the Mount, Jesus' advice to settle a legal dispute as quickly as possible seems to be a reference to settling an outstanding debt (Mt 5:23-26). In this teaching, the threat of debt, just as in the Old Testament, is loss of freedom. In Paul's letter to the Romans, the apostle provides a long series of instruction (chapters 12 and 13) about how the community of believers is to conduct itself in relation to the broader world, reminding them that they represent the body of Christ in the world, called to sacrificial living (Rom 12:1) and overcoming evil with good (Rom 12:21). Just as with Israel in the Old Testament, they are called to be witnesses to the reign of God. As part of this overall vocation of witness, Paul emphasises in chapter 13 that the believers should have *no outstanding obligations* against them, summing up: 'Owe no one anything, except to love one another' (Rom 13:8). In the New Testament, just as in the Old, we are called to freedom, not just for itself, but so we are *free to follow God*.

How Might We Respond?

Clearly, the Old Testament laws about debt remission and Jubilee are not particularly applicable to modern Christian thinking about debt. It would not be advisable to ask your bank manager to cancel your mortgage after seven years. However, the Bible's general principles and understanding of debt are still instructive: (i) that debt may well be necessary at some points in life, but; (ii) it is generally a state to be avoided or settled as quickly as possible. For us, as with the ancients, the core question is one of who we are obligated to serve and whether we are truly free to follow God.

Housing debt

The basic issue of housing is a good example of a situation where debt may indeed be a necessary evil for most people. Nevertheless, there is more scope to think critically and creatively about this area of life than has often been acknowledged.

In Australia, we are generally limited to two sorts of housing choices: renting on the private rental market or buying a house. In a few places there is a third option of housing cooperatives, which provide affordable housing with long-term security of tenancy – an excellent option for those who can get it. Often, people have ideologically predisposed attitudes as to which form of housing is more legitimate: the majority of people assume that owning your own home should be the goal of life, while a very few others, who are critical of this attitude and of social inequality, have come to see home ownership as wrong. Neither of these attitudes is particularly helpful to a constructive weighing of the principles and practicalities involved in housing.

On the whole, owning your own home does seem preferable to renting for a host of reasons: the money being paid monthly towards housing is going towards an asset that belongs to the family, rather than paying off someone else's investment; it is more secure than renting; and it makes possible all sorts of alterations to the house and property for the sake of sustainability (see chapter 3) that are generally not possible in rentals. The major drawback of home ownership is that it usually requires entering into a very substantial debt.

The question is not whether it is good or bad to go into debt, but rather, *what is the cost of our housing choices?* And when we think about cost, we need to go well beyond thinking of financial cost, to consider what impact our choices will have on our work and vocation, family and broader community involvement (see chapter 1), low consumption and sustainable lifestyles (chapters 2 and 3) and giving (chapter 4). The tragedy of so many Christian folk with visions of serving God is that they decided on a mortgage based on calculations that suggested they could just 'afford' it, without thinking about what the true cost was in terms of time commitments, relationships and the freedom to follow God.

Once a broad consideration of the costs is in view, then choices about housing become less pre-determined and more dependent on how the different options stack up against each other. This is something that is obviously dependent on particular circumstances and must be done on a case-by-case basis. However, it does suggest a number of things:

1. What is being weighed primarily is the weekly mortgage repayment against the weekly cost of rental. Mortgage repayments should be calculated with the consideration that interest rates could rise (allowing an extra 2 per cent is

usually recommended), whereas rental repayments should be considered with a view of the particular local rental market – is rent rising quickly? Is rental secure or insecure?

2. The size and type of housing has a huge impact on the price, whether buying or renting; the more we can adjust our expectations towards smaller, simpler housing, the less impact housing costs will have on the rest of our lives.

3. *Where* you live is also a huge determinant of cost; if Christians want to live in affluent suburbs, the cost of this choice will flow through to all areas of their lives. On the other hand, there are a bunch of good reasons why Christians should consider clustering in less affluent areas (see chapter 1), of which the lower cost of housing is but one.

Although generally it seems preferable to own your own home, this should not be a goal at any cost. If Christians are serious about following God with their whole lives, then there will be times when the cost of a mortgage should be judged as too high. Following such principles may well require waiting longer until the time is right, which is a scary prospect for some, or thinking about housing altogether differently.

If the choice is being made to seek credit to buy a house, it is worth giving some thought to thinking about where the money will come from. There are two reasons for this: (i) to be seeking terms and rates that make the debt the least onerous as possible; and (ii) if you are going to be paying interest, to be asking to whom that money is going and for what it is going to be used. Here, the discussion about banks, member-owned banks and credit unions in chapter 6 becomes relevant and the same principles apply: it is better to seek credit in member-owned and community-owned institutions where the money will be recycled within the community, rather than siphoned off into the global financial market.

However, it is also worth inquiring as to whether there are any alternative sources of credit outside of the standard financial institutions. The first port of call for thinking about this is usually family and it is entirely natural and appropriate that the housing affordability crisis has forced many families to work cooperatively with their financial resources. This can be done through parents advancing their children's inheritance (or a portion of it), low interest loans within the family, joint purchasing arrangements, or a mix of all three. Depending on family context, such schemes are not without pitfalls, so it is important to give it careful consideration first.

Beyond the family, it *should* also be natural to turn to the broader church community for financial assistance. Churches are the perfect place for creative initiatives in cooperative credit (see chapter 6). However, such schemes are unfortunately very rare. This is a hole that is waiting to be filled by some creative and kingdom-minded accountants ...

Credit cards

There is no doubt that the flexibility and utility of Visa and MasterCard is a convenience to which we have become accustomed. However, seen from the alternative biblical worldview that we have been trying to inhabit, credit cards are a really bad idea. Their whole purpose is to loosen the bonds of restraint, to encourage frivolous expenditure or to bring forward expenditure that would otherwise have required waiting and saving. They stimulate the urge towards self-gratification and dissolve the discipline of patience. Credit cards have given major impetus to a culture of excessive consumption (chapter 2) and have played a large part in the mounting financial pressure on families, including trapping some families into employment patterns that they otherwise might not have chosen. Credit cards are a gilt-edged form of bondage, but bondage nonetheless.

The best option for most people would be simply to abandon credit cards. They simply should not be necessary. These days, you can still have the convenience of a Visa and MasterCard that functions merely as a *debit* card tied to a savings account. This means you are only paying for things with money you actually have. If we cannot conceive of actually *living within our means*, then we have given ourselves over to the spirit of consumerism.

In the place that is vacated by the credit card, we should institute three revolutionary practices:

i. Budgeting: If the idea of getting through weekly or monthly expenditure without a credit card seems terrifying, then this is a sure sign of a failure in budgeting. This is a simple practice that seems to have become distasteful to many people, but it is hard to emphasise how important budgeting is to instituting some sort of ethical framework to household economics. There are different ways of budgeting and they don't all have to be microscopic or tedious processes, but whichever one you use, all budgeting is essentially a process of trying to come to grips with household income and household expenditure and trying to make the two match.

ii. Waiting: If it is not *necessary*, and you do not have the money, just wait, budget and save. This has a couple of benefits: it allows the immediate desire for a particular thing to be subjected to a bit more critical scrutiny over time and it forces you to weigh that thing in relation to other expenditures.

iii. Doing without: What! This seems unthinkable in our consumer culture. However, learning not to be shaped by the desire for what everyone else seems to have, but rather accepting with gratitude what one does have, is at the very heart of the gospel's teaching about material things (see chapter 2). Learning to do without is the secret of contentment amidst the frenzy of hyper-consumption.

If, for whatever reason, you absolutely must have a credit card, then the challenge is to try to transform your mental attitude to it. Whereas we have been encouraged to think of credit cards as friends and given them pride of place in our wallets, it would be better, if you must have a credit card, to bury it in your wallet and to try to view it as a necessary evil, to be used reluctantly and sparingly.

Examples of steps people have taken

- Change your credit card to a debit card.

- Begin using a 'credit card condom', (a sleeve on your credit card reminding you to think about whether you really need to use it, or whether you really need the article).
- If you have multiple debts, look into the option of consolidating (refinancing) your debts into a single debt that reduces your interest burden and repayment stress.
- If you have no debt, educate yourself on the effect of how debt is working in people's lives and the economy – seek to read a book or some articles on the subject.
- If you are considering buying a house, think carefully about the size, quality and location of that housing, and what sort of mortgage that will require.

Conclusion

The church of modern times has had very little to say about the basic economic structures of our households. Christian faith has been so privatised and spiritualised that the vision and values underpinning the material ordering of our lives have largely been left to be moulded by an all-pervasive consumer culture. And so Christians in the affluent West have been led blindfolded into an economic way of life that is destructive of creation and human dignity, that acts as a solvent for the bonds of family and community, and that is founded upon a nihilistic pursuit of individual gratification. Essentially, we have ended up trying to serve two masters, and that, as Jesus explains, is something that simply cannot be done. The result is evident in the crisis of faith that besets Christianity in the West.

Attempting to reclaim a Christian practice of household economy, therefore, has a manifold purpose. Firstly, it is an ethical response to the destructive economics of our time that joins the dots and locates our own personal implication within the system. Seen aright, it is not motivated by a need to be 'free from the taint of sin' but rather by a desire to show care for our neighbours and for the earth; that is, it is driven by deep yearning to see right done – what the Bible calls *righteousness*. Beginning to reshape our own household practices in relation to climate change or worker exploitation is not, in and of itself, *a solution* to these problems – so much more is required – but represents a basic Christian commitment to seek right relationship and to *be* the change we want to see in the world. That is partly what the New Testament means when it speaks of the people of God as the first-fruits of the age to come. This is a movement towards the integration of what we believe, what we hope for and how we act; that is, it is a movement towards *integrity* or, in the deeper and fuller language of the Bible, it is a movement towards *holiness*.

Secondly, beginning to reshape the material ordering of our lives is a way of simply trying to *see more clearly* in an age of confusion, seduction and deception. Where we stand determines what we see and our ability to see through some of the core lies and idolatries of our time – 'more is better', 'there is no alternative', 'I have to do what is right for me' – is to a very large extent dependent on beginning to re-position ourselves in relation to them. For the Apostle Paul, our ability to 'discern what is the will of God' or even 'what is *good*' is predicated on firstly presenting our bodies – that is, our physical and material existence – as living sacrifices and conforming no longer to 'the pattern of this present world' (Rom 12:1-2, REB). Beginning to re-order our material lives is part of what is required to allow us to better hear and comprehend the immensity of the good news of Jesus and thus to make us more effective bearers of that good news into the world.

Finally, jumping off the highway of 'business as usual' is the essential condition of living well in an age of bad living. The reason the Bible locates non-conformity as an essential condition of holiness – that is, of *wholeness*, in the fullest sense – is not because God wants an exclusive club of the holy, but because, in a fallen and fractured world, non-conformity is the essential condition of health. The startling truth is that the world-inverting message of Jesus really is *good news*, not just for the age to come, but here and now. Our ability to bear good news to the world is linked to our own *experience* of that good news. In the end, God calls us to re-order our material lives in right relationship to himself, to our neighbours and to creation because that is precisely where we will find fullness of life. In the economy of God, salvation, holiness, justice and evangelism are all merely different adjectives describing the same big idea.

We must also come to terms, of course, with the fact that all of our efforts to re-order our material lives – our concern for the other, our endeavour to see more clearly, our experience of good news – are only ever provisional and partial. The world is just so big and complex, life gets so messy and we are so prone to weakness and venality of one sort or another. We can never quite shake the monkey from our shoulder. But this is where the beauty of the gospel comes into its own, for this is precisely the human reality that is taken for granted when, *nonetheless*, the God who is in Christ invites us to participate in another reality where God's will is done: the kingdom of God. We do not need to get everything right or even attain a certain level of 'goodness' as an entry point; all we are called to do is to come to the deep recognition of our need for God. 'Blessed are the poor in spirit, for theirs is the kingdom of heaven' (Mt 5:3).

This book has attempted to describe a movement towards a Christian practice of household economy. Hopefully, it should be clear that such a thing cannot be prescribed. It cannot be reduced to a set of rules and practices that constitute 'the right way to live'. While I have attempted throughout this book to provide concrete *examples* of ways in which some have attempted to flesh out a principle, such examples should emphatically not be taken as *the* way that Christians should live within the 21st century affluent world. For one thing, our globalised world is so complex that very often the most ethical or sustainable course of action is not clear. We are continually confronted with the need to act in the face of some uncertainty, attempting to make the best choices we can based on the best information we have. When the best information changes (as it will), then we need to be ready to change our choices. And thus we see that a Christian practice of household economy is not some easily definable end point, but rather a journey. It cannot be founded on the certainty of being right, but rather must be founded on the *habit* of allowing the love of God, neighbour and creation to continually shape our lives, as best we can.

To do this, however, we do need to be clear about the *principles* by which the people of God are called to live. Even better, we need to be clear about the *spirit* through which we are called to live. It is here that the Bible can be much more of a living Word than we have generally allowed it to be. Throughout this book, I have endeavoured to show that the Bible contains a wealth of teaching about how we order our material lives that is based both on a penetrating understanding of human fallenness and a consistent vision of what wholeness requires.

While our own particular circumstances are a world away from those circumstances being addressed in the Bible, again and again we find that the underlying issues and tendencies being addressed are strikingly familiar. In each of the seven areas discussed in this book, we find the Bible has identified ways in which our conduct can do harm to our relationships with God, with each other and with the earth, and it has consistently exhorted action in the contrary direction: towards *restoring* relationship with God, with each other and with the earth. Although the particularities of these exhortations may not be applicable to our context, there is an underlying consistency of spirit and principle in the Bible's teaching that can be extended into our own post-modern globalised consumer society. We are given sure guidance as to the shape of both temptation and healing, but we must ourselves undertake the creative, spiritual and intellectual wrestling to apply this to our own contexts. This is indeed the process of Word becoming flesh in our lives. The gospel – the good news that God speaks to us – must always be translated into the messiness of human life. It is not an abstract or ethereal message, but rather a message with real content for our lives here and now, trapped as we are in the web of human brokenness.

> Surely, this commandment that I am commanding you today is not too hard for you, nor is it too far away. [...] No, *the word is very near to you*; it is in your mouth and in your heart for you to observe. See, I have set before you today life and prosperity, death and adversity. ... Choose life (Deut 30:11-15, 19b)

What needs to be emphasised once again in the final paragraphs of this book is that the movement towards a Christian practice of household economy is a journey and not an end point. It is, in fact, the work of the rest of our lives and it will never be finished. This is important because everyone begins this journey from a different starting point. The huge differences in contexts, circumstances and capabilities between various households means it is not possible to make simple prescriptions, even were such a thing desirable. What is possible for each of us differs enormously, but we can all take a step. There is much wisdom in the Taoist saying, 'The journey of a thousand miles must begin with a single step'. God is not interested in the level of our advancement, but rather in the direction of our travel. He is not interested in perfection, but rather the next step.

To this end, some readers may find the Household Covenant described in Appendix 1 to be a useful tool for making steps towards change in the practice of household economy. The virtue of this tool is that all steps must be self-identified; it simply provides the framework for making clearly definable changes. But this is also the burden. As Jacob knew, there is no blessing in the life of faith without great struggle. In the end, it is incumbent on all of us to personally undertake the spiritual and intellectual wrestling that is required if we are to align ourselves to Christ. It is to this that we are called.

Appendices

The Household Covenant as a Tool for Change

The Household Covenant in a nutshell.

1. Write down at least one goal for a change your household will seek to make in each of the seven areas, over the next 12 months.
2. At the end of the 12 months, re-visit your goals and see how you went.
3. Set new goals (or renew old ones) for the next 12 months.

The Household Covenant is simply a tool for making choices towards a more responsible way of living; it is not an end in itself. It should be emphasised that there is no 'right' way of using the covenant, no goals you must meet, and no particular targets to achieve. At its most basic level, it simply provides a process for helping us to think about various areas of our lives and bringing God and the Bible into that thinking. However, the Household Covenant also brings the opportunity to try to make some practical changes that better reflect the life we are called to in Christ. The challenge is to name one goal in each area that you can work towards over the next year.

The process of the Covenant is one of thinking biblically and involves three steps:

1. Attempting to see the world clearly. In each area of the Covenant, we begin by asking, 'What's the problem here?'
2. Hearing God's voice through the Bible. What principles does the Bible teach in each area of the Covenant?
3. Translating the biblical message into our contexts. What practical changes can we begin to make?

This process is best undertaken in groups, as a great deal of value comes out of different peoples' perspectives, ideas and knowledge; however, it can certainly be used individually as well. A Household Covenant Bible Study Guide can be downloaded for free from the

website of Manna Gum at www.mannagum.org.au/faith_and_economy/
the_household_covenant

Making and Renewing Household Covenant Goals

The challenge of the Household Covenant is to name one goal in each
area that you can work towards over the next year. Household Covenant
goals might be modest baby steps or big, hairy ambitious ones, or you
might have a mix of both. The key is to try to name goals that are *actually
attainable*. Every household's circumstances, capacities and life seasons
are different, and these will shape what goals are possible for each; what
might seem easy to some might be completely unattainable for others.
The challenge is for everyone to try to name *something*. I recommend
you write your goals down and date them.

After a year, return to your goals and see how you went. If you felt
you achieved them, then set yourself some new goals for the next year.
If you felt you didn't do so well, ask yourself why. Perhaps your goals
were unrealistic, did not suit your context, your life circumstances
changed, or perhaps you were just a bit slack. Whatever the case, you
have a chance to reformulate your goals – either new ones or the same
ones again – for the coming year. Try to be specific rather than vague.
For example, rather than 'Goal: use less water' do something like 'Goal:
reduce household water consumption from 400 litres/day to 300 litres/
day'. Making a goal measurable lets you know how you are going towards
achieving it.

Many people will find that there is one area of the Covenant where
they just don't know what to do, either because it seems too hard or it
is just not relevant (e.g. if you don't have any debt). In these cases, a
goal might be as simple as deciding to read a book, article or find out
some information on the subject. You never know, in future years your
circumstances or perspective may change, and this area might become
more relevant or more attainable. In some areas, you might feel that you
can accomplish more than one goal over a year. Nothing wrong with
that. For those renewing goals, it may seem appropriate in one or two
areas to keep the same goal as last year ongoing. Nothing wrong with

that either. If you later decide that the goal you have set is not going to work for some reason, then just re-evaluate and change it. Nothing wrong with that either. Remember, the Covenant is only a tool.

OUR HOUSEHOLD COVENANT

For the household of		
Area	**Goal**	**Date**
1. Hospitality		
2. Work & Leisure		
3. Consumption		
4. Sustainability		
5. Giving		
6. Savings & Investment		
7. Debt		

Money and the Misuse of Scripture: Revisiting the Stewardship Parables

In 2000, Brian Houston, pastor of Hillsong Church, published a book entitled *You Need More Money*. In his introduction he quotes a text from Ecclesiastes – 'A feast is made for laughter, and wine makes merry; but money answers everything' (10:19) – and then observes: 'If that's a shock to see a statement like that in the Bible—check it out for yourself. That is exactly what it says: MONEY ANSWERS EVERYTHING!' For Houston, this obscure text from one of the more difficult Old Testament books (which also contains multiple texts in contradiction of this sentiment) somehow becomes the basis for an entire Christian theology of money. (Houston has since publicly regretted publishing this book, but not necessarily its underlying ideas.)

Brian Houston is something of an easy target for people outraged by misuses of the Bible, but the more uncomfortable truth is that his ability to screen out almost everything that Jesus teaches about money is fairly widespread across the Christian church. Since the time of the Protestant Reformation, there have consistently been those who have somehow seen in Christianity a justification for the pursuit of wealth. How can this be?

There are some common mis-readings of the gospels on the matter of money, and foremost among these is the way in which we have mis-read and misused the 'Stewardship' Parables, by which I mean the Parable of the Talents (Mt 25:14-30) and the Parable of the Minas (or Pounds, depending on your translation) (Lk 19:11-27).

The Stewardship Parables are among the more well-known of Jesus' parables, and they are one of the few of Jesus' teachings on money that are likely to be regularly preached from the pulpit, especially on 'Stewardship Sunday'. The basic story, common to both, seems simple enough: a rich nobleman goes away on a journey and entrusts a sum of money to three servants. Two of the servants gainfully invest the money, making a profit for their employer, and for this they are duly rewarded when he returns. The third does nothing with the money and cops it.

There are generally two variants of interpretation of this parable:

1. We should use our 'talents' (that is, the gifts and abilities we have been endowed with) to serve God as best we can;

2. We should invest our money so that it is continually making a return. This is prudent 'stewardship' of the financial resources with which God has entrusted us. Many have even gone so far as to argue that this teaching provides a Christian justification of capitalism.

Often these two interpretations come packaged together, and in both interpretations, the rich nobleman is Jesus, and we are the servants. Seems pretty straightforward, doesn't it?

Most Christians implicitly accept these readings without question; the *interpretation* of the text has almost become as much an article of faith as the text itself. Nevertheless, in my experience, when paying proper attention to the text, many people are also vaguely uncomfortable about the whole thing. Something doesn't sit quite right. How is it that the Jesus who earlier denounced mammon is now telling us to make lots of money? And if the nobleman is Jesus, how do we square his brutality with the picture of Jesus we get in the rest of the gospels? If only we paid more attention to these vaguely articulated discomforts when we read the Bible …

Actually, there is an entirely different way of reading this story that sits much more comfortably and consistently within the teachings of Jesus and the gospel narrative as a whole. But to get a clearer sense of this, we need to pay closer attention to the fact that there are indeed *two* stories, one in Matthew and one in Luke, and while they are basically the same, they also hold some subtle but important differences. One of the main differences is the denominations of money entrusted to the slaves: in Matthew the first slave is given 5 *talents* (2 to the second, and one to the last), which is a ludicrously exorbitant amount of money equivalent to 75 years wages for a day labourer. In Luke's account he gives the servants 10 *minas* ('pounds' in many translations), equivalent to 2½ year's wages.

For some reason, Matthew's Parable of the Talents is by far the most well-known – perhaps because it contains the word 'talents', even though it actually has nothing to do with our English word referring to gifts or abilities. A 'talent' here is merely the proper name for a coinage. However, although it is rarely acknowledged, in many ways Matthew's story is a much more difficult and enigmatic story. Matthew has his story set amidst the judgements teachings of chapter 25 (following the Parable of the Ten Bridesmaids and preceding the account of the sheep and the goats) and how this positioning influences the reading of the Parable of the Talents is by no means a straightforward matter. Then the text itself seems to throw some confusing signals as to how we should be reading the story. Perhaps because of this difficult and enigmatic character, people have tended to suppress their questions about how it is to be interpreted.

Why haven't we noticed that none of these difficulties apply to Luke's story of the minas? Once we pay attention to it, everything about Luke's telling of the story and its placement within the overall gospel narrative makes it blindingly obvious that the dominant interpretation, so widely accepted, cannot possibly apply.

Luke's story of the minas is introduced with a very particular context that Luke wants us to keep in mind: 'he went on to tell a parable, *because he was near Jerusalem*, and *because they supposed* that the kingdom of God was to appear immediately' (19:11). They are getting close to the place where Jesus will be killed by the authorities, and Jesus is painfully aware that his disciples have completely false expectations about what is going to happen there. As Cleopas later confesses on the road to Emmaus, 'we had hoped that he was the one to redeem Israel' (24:21), by which he means that they thought Jesus would liberate them from the Romans and restore the Davidic kingship.

Very importantly, Luke does not begin the story with 'The kingdom of God is like ...'. This is not one of Jesus' famous kingdom parables, it is a story about something else. We have become accustomed to reading all parables through one interpretive lens, when they actually are a quite diverse collection of teachings. As William Herzog has pointed out, rather than being 'earthly stories with heavenly meanings', they are often 'earthy stories with heavy meanings'.

So Jesus tells them a story about 'A nobleman [who] went to a distant country to get royal power for himself and then return' (19:12). He also pointedly lets us know that 'the citizens of his country hated him and sent a delegation after him, saying, 'We do not want this man to rule over us.' (19:14). Here we should be alerted that this is not a heavenly story. As Jesus listeners were well aware, this was precisely how both Herod the Great, and then his heir, Archelaus, rose to become rulers of Judaea by appealing to Rome, against the opposition of their countrymen. Herod and Archelaus were both remembered as notoriously brutal and unpopular kings.

This unpopular nobleman appoints ten slaves (many translations have 'servants', but 'slaves' is more accurate) and divides ten minas among them, instructing them 'to do business with it' until his return. Upon his triumphal return, now as a king, he summons the slaves back to give an account of their dealings. The first reports that his investment of the mina has earned the king another ten minas, a fantastical return on investment of 1000 per cent, while the second reports a 500 per cent rate of return! These two 'good slaves' are rewarded by being given rule over a number of cities commensurate with their financial success.

The third slave comes forward (for some reason we don't hear about the remaining seven) and returns the mina to the king, reporting that he did nothing with it but 'wrapped it up in a piece of cloth' (19:20). In the usual interpretation of this parable we are accustomed to seeing the third slave as lazy, apathetic, or unwilling to take risks. However, the reason he actually gives for his inaction is electrifying, and something that should make us sit up and take notice: 'I was afraid of you, because you are a harsh man; you take what you did not deposit and reap what you did not sow' (19:21). This slave shines light on the fact that this new king's wealth (and presumably the incredible profits of the other two slaves) has been built upon dispossessing others. Despite acknowledging his fear of the king, he has named him to his face!

The king is outraged at this insolence, but, curiously, entirely accepts the third slave's description of him: 'You wicked slave! You knew, did you, that I was a harsh man, taking what I did not deposit and reaping what I did not sow? Why then did you not put my money into the bank? Then when I returned, I could have collected it with interest' (19:22-23).

Bank? Which bank? There is no such thing as a bank in ancient Judea and won't be for over a thousand years. This is a trick of the translation into English. The actual word used (*trapeza*) refers to the table of the money changers. It is the same tables that Jesus will go and overturn in the Temple at the end of this very same chapter!

Collected interest? The charging of interest from a countryman is one of the most repugnant acts forbidden in the Hebrew Torah (see Ex 22:25, Lev 25:35-37 and Deut 23:19-20). It was seen as a primary driver of dispossession, poverty and bondage, and thus understood as quintessentially oppressive and exploitative. And indeed, the time of Jesus was precisely a time of growing landlessness among the poor and huge consolidations of land by the wealthy elite, all driven by debt. Earlier in Luke, Jesus has instructed his followers to go further than loaning without interest and to lend *without expecting repayment*! (Lk 6:34-35)

The king then goes on to fully confirm the third slave's assessment of him: 'Take the pound from him and give it to the one who has ten pounds.' (And they said to him, 'Lord, he has ten pounds!') 'I tell you, to all those who have, more will be given; but from those who have nothing, even what they have will be taken away. But as for these enemies of mine who did not want me to be king over them— bring them here and slaughter them in my presence' (19:24-27).

By this point we should be seriously wondering how it is that we have interpreted this as an allegory in which Jesus is the king. In telling this story, Jesus has piled up negative signals, each the exact opposite of the kingdom he has been proclaiming throughout the gospel. This is not a story of the kingdom of God but of the kingdoms of the world and how they really work. We have taken the verse – 'I tell you, to all those who have, more will be given; but from those who have nothing, even what they have will be taken away' – and we have entirely spiritualised it to somehow extract a positive theological message, without noticing that this is what has been happening in the world throughout history: the poor are dispossessed of what they have and the wealthy get wealthier. It was one of the major social phenomena of the time of Jesus, it is something I have witnessed time and again in the Mekong region, and it is what Thomas Piketty confirmed through his enormous assemblage of economic data in *Capital in the Twenty-First Century*.

When viewed from this perspective, we begin to see the third slave in a new light. He is the one who spoke truth to power and paid the price for it. Remember that this story is introduced by telling us Jesus is heading to Jerusalem, the place where he knew he would be executed by the powers. And remember that he told this story to his disciples because 'they supposed the kingdom of God was to appear immediately' when he got to Jerusalem. If Jesus is anyone in this story, he is the third slave. He has spoken the truth and he will pay the price.

Finally, and most exasperatingly, to be able to somehow interpret this parable as a teaching in which Jesus is commending lucrative financial investments, we have to pretend that the rest of the Gospel of Luke does not exist. Of all the gospels, this is the one that most strongly and consistently sounds a strong warning against the dangers of accumulating wealth. This is such an important point it is worth a brief recap of what Jesus has already said concerning money in Luke (see table below).

	Texts on Money & Wealth in the Gospel of Luke
6:24	'Woe to you who are rich'.
6:27-36	Give to everyone who begs from you; lend expecting no return.
8:14	In the Parable of the Sower: 'As for what fell among the thorns, these are the ones who hear; but as they go on their way, they are choked by the cares and riches and pleasures of life, and their fruit does not mature.'
11:3-4	The Lord's Prayer: 'Give us this day our daily bread, forgive us our sins as we forgive everyone indebted to us'.
12:13-21	The Parable of the Rich Fool who increased the size of his storehouses: 'And God said to him 'You fool!''
12:22-31	'Do not keep striving for what you are to eat and what you are to drink, and do not keep worrying. … Instead, strive for his kingdom, and these things will be given you as well.'
12:33-34	'Sell your possessions and give alms. Make purses for yourselves that do not wear out, and unfailing treasure in heaven, where no thief comes near and no moth destroys. For where your treasure is, there your heart will be also.'
14:33	'None of you can become my disciple if you do not give up all your possessions'.
16:9	'make *friends* for yourselves by means of dishonest wealth [*mammon*] so that when it is gone, they may welcome you into the eternal homes.'
16:13	'No slave can serve two masters; for a slave will either hate the one and love the other, or be devoted to the one and despise the other. You cannot serve God and wealth.'

16:14-15	'The Pharisees, who were lovers of money, heard all this, and they ridiculed him. So he said to them, "You are those who justify yourselves in the sight of others; but God knows your hearts; for what is prized by human beings is an abomination in the sight of God."
16:19-31	The Parable of the Rich Man and Lazarus: 'Child, remember that during your lifetime you received your good things, and Lazarus in like manner evil things; but now he is comforted here, and you are in agony.'
18:18-28	The encounter with the rich ruler: 'Sell all that you own and distribute the money to the poor, and you will have treasure in heaven; then come, follow me.' But when he heard this, he became sad; for he was very rich. Jesus looked at him and said, 'How hard it is for those who have wealth to enter the kingdom of God! Indeed, it is easier for a camel to go through the eye of a needle than for someone who is rich to enter the kingdom of God.'
19:1-10	[The story immediately preceding the Parable of the Minas] The story of Zacchaeus who repents of his unjust wealth, giving half his possessions to the poor and repaying those he defrauded fourfold.
19:11-27	The Parable of the Minas.
19:45-48	Jesus turns over the tables of the moneychangers in the Temple, quoting Jeremiah: 'My house shall be a house of prayer, but you have made it a den of robbers'.

As a whole, Luke's Gospel presents a consistently devastating critique of money and wealth, and especially the chapters directly preceding the Parable of the Minas. Let me stress: this is not a simple and straightforward subject. How we, the products of a vastly wealthy consumer society, practically make sense of such teachings, is an enormously difficult task that requires great intellectual and spiritual wrestling, and the slow unravelling of layers of complexity. For now, the simple point I want to make is that it is entirely inconceivable that following all of what has preceded in the Gospel of Luke, Jesus could, in the Parable of the Minas, suddenly be advocating the accumulation of wealth as responsible discipleship, what we have often euphemistically meant by the term 'stewardship'. Jesus is categorically *not* saying, 'You need more money'. The fact that this parable has indeed been interpreted in this way should give us serious pause about the ways in which we have read and used the Bible.

What about Matthew's Parable of the Talents? In Matthew's story the negative signals about the master (not a king in this version) and the nature and process of 'investment' described above also apply, however, they are a more mixed set of signals and not as resoundingly clear as in Luke's version. Moreover, it might be argued that the placement in Matthew in amidst a series of teachings on being prepared for the return of Jesus (the Parable of the Ten Bridesmaids) and a teaching on judgement (the sheep and the goats), and the fact that the person in power in both the parable of the bridesmaids and the sheep and the goats is clearly God, both seem to weigh in favour of the traditional allegorical reading in which God is the master in the story. But then again, the climax of this cycle of teaching with the judgement of the sheep and the goats – where judgement is explicitly predicated on what we did for 'the least of these' – makes it hard to believe Matthew was condoning usury in the preceding story. In fact, whichever way you choose to read it – whether the traditional allegorical interpretation or the inverted reading I have suggested for Luke's parable of the minas – Matthew's Parable of the Talents is an uncomfortably enigmatic story with elements that don't quite sit right.

I think that it is possible that Matthew did understand the parable in quite a different light from Luke, and *perhaps* he did intend the traditional allegorical interpretation. I am personally agnostic on this, as neither interpretation answers all objections. However, what is nevertheless clear is that if you opt for an allegorical reading of Matthew's story, then the reading must be treated *entirely* allegorically and not as a teaching about money ('stewardship') at all. Matthew has the same basic teachings on money as Luke and to imagine that he is here commending lucrative investments requires pretending the rest of Matthew's gospel doesn't exist, just as with Luke.

Whichever way you go, Matthew's Parable of the Talents is just a difficult passage. What is clear is that if we are looking for a teaching on *money*, then the clarity of Luke's parable of the minas – not to mention all the rest of Jesus' teachings on money throughout *both* gospels – must override any uncertainties about this one parable in Matthew.

Lightning Source UK Ltd.
Milton Keynes UK
UKHW021213211019
352003UK00011B/2267/P